Dear Jeanne,

A memento of your short visit
to San Fernando.

Love and Best Wishes

from Ingrid and Purley

March 2010

TRINIDAD AND TOBAGO
TERRIFIC AND TRANQUIL

SECOND EDITION

EDITED BY ARIF ALI

HANSIB

Published in Great Britain in 2006
Hansib Publications Limited
London & Hertfordshire, UK

Email: info@hansib-books.com
Website: www.hansib-books.com

ISBN 1 870518 80 2

Cover designed by Kash and Lucy Ali

Design and Production by Books of Colour, Hertfordshire, UK

Printed and bound by Butler and Tanner, Frome & London, UK

*Established in 1850, Butler and Tanner is the UK's leading book and brochure printer, with
multiple awards for exceptional quality. They are one of the greenest printing outfits in the world*

Contents

HANSIB PUBLICATIONS IS GRATEFUL TO THE FOLLOWING BUSINESSES AND ORGANISATIONS FOR THEIR SUPPORT

International dialling code for Trinidad and Tobago: 868

BP Trinidad and Tobago
5-5a Queen's Park West
Port of Spain
Tel: 623 2862
Fax: 627 7863

Brandsville
88-90 Pike Street
Section 'M' Campbelville
Georgetown
GUYANA
Tel: 226 1133, 226 6162
Fax: 231 7001
Email:
brandsville@gol.net.gy

Caribbean Discovery Tours Ltd
9B Fondes Amandes Road
St Ann's
Port of Spain

Tel: 624 7281
Fax: 624 8596

Charrans Bookstores
53 Eastern Main Road
Tunapuna

Tel: 663 1884/ 645 3878
Fax: 645 8315
Email:
hennycharran@hotmail.com

Courts (Trinidad) Ltd
Megastore Complex
Churchill Roosevelt
Highway
San Juan
Tel: 674 5409
Fax: 674 6667

Crown Point Beach Hotel Ltd
PO Box 223, Scarborough
Tobago
Tel: 639 8781
Fax: 639 8731
Email:
crownpoint@sunsurfsand.com

CWC World Cup (2007) T & T Ltd
5th Floor, Tatil Building
11 Maraval Road
Port of Spain
Tel: 628 9314
Fax: 622 5424
Email:
info.trinidadandtobago
@cricketworldcup.com

eTeck
The Atrium
Don Miguel Road Extension
El Socorro
Tel: 675 1989
Email: info@eteck.co.tt

Ishmael Khan
20 Henry Street
Port of Spain
Tel: 623 4523
Fax: 625 7996
Email:
imkhanpos@tstt.net.tt

Kanhai Real Estate
242 North Stars Avenue
Malabar, Phase 2, Arima
Tel/Fax: 642 7375

Keith Khan's Books Etc, Ltd
58 Frederick Street
Port of Spain
Tel: 623 1201
Email: kkhan@tstt.net.tt

Lexicon Trinidad Ltd
LP#48 Boundary Road
San Juan
Tel: 675 3389
Fax: 675 3395
Email: lexicon@tstt.net.tt

Metropolitan Book Suppliers Limited
Capital Plaza
11-13 Frederick Street
Port of Spain
Tel/Fax: 623 3462
Fax: 627 0856
Email:
metrobooksuppliers@tstt.net.tt

MovieTowne Mall & Cineplex Multicinemas Trinidad Ltd
Lot D, MovieTowne
Boulevard
Audrey Jeffers Highway
Port of Spain
Tel: 627 8277
Fax: 625 9552
Email:
info@movietowne.com

National Gas Company of Trinidad and Tobago Ltd
Orinoco Drive
Point Lisas Industrial Estate
Point Lisas
Box 1127 Port of Spain
Tel: 636 4662/4680
Fax: 679 2384
Email: info@ngc.co.tt

Neal & Massy Group
63 Park Street
Port of Spain
Tel: 625 3426
Fax: 627 9061
Email: nmh@neal-and-massy.com

R.I.K. Services Limited (Trinidad Book World)
104 High Street
San Fernando
Tel: 652 4824
Fax: 657 6793
Email: rik@carib-link.net

& 7 Queen Street
Port of Spain
Tel: 623 4316

Ross Advertising Image Consultancy & Events Management
16 Gray Street, St Clair
Port of Spain
Tel: 622 1967/622 4306/628 0450
Fax: 622 1779
Email:
ross@rossadvertising.co.tt

SUEZ LNG (Trinidad and Tobago) Ltd
1st Floor, Chamber of
Commerce Building –
Columbus Circle
Westmoorings
Tel: 633 1919
Fax: 633 2020

The Falls at Westmall
Western Main Road
Westmoorings
Tel: 632 1239
Fax: 633 1245

Trinidad and Tobago Sightseeing Tours
#12 Western Main Road
St James
Port of Spain
Tel: 628 1051
Fax: 622 9205
Email: carvalho@tstt.net.tt

Acknowledgements

Thank you to the following for their help and support towards the publication of *Trinidad and Tobago: Terrific and Tranquil*.

First of all to Minister of Tourism, Howard Chin-Lee; President and Director of Tourism Development Company Limited (TDC), Dr James R Hepple; and Chairman of TDC, Charles Carvalho, for commissioning the project.

To our UK team: **Managing Editor, Kash Ali**; Project Co-ordinator, Isha Persaud; Richard Painter, Ella Barnes, Alan Cross, and our printers, Butler and Tanner.

In Trinidad and Tobago: To our Co-ordinating Editor, Dr Kris Rampersad, whose commitment was invaluable to the project; to Stephen Broadbridge, for his sterling effort; to Nicole du Boulet, Candice Ali, Charlene Sealy, Indul Kanhai, Lorraine Pouchet, Elton Pouchet, Hugh Ferreira, Peter Kanhai, Fidel Persaud, Kailash Bedi, Angie Benjamin, Kendrick Sooknarine, Claire Broadbridge, Wayne Richardson, Chandani Persaud, Peter Kanhai; to the management and staff at the Hilton Hotel; to the management and staff at the Chancellor Hotel; to the BWIA staff in London and Trinidad; and Insight Guides, for the map of Trinidad and Tobago.

To the writers (in alphabetical order): Louis Araujo, Sita Bridgemohan, Elspeth Duncan, Simon Lee, Denzil Mohammed, Fazeer Mohammed, Kris Rampersad

To the photographers (in alphabetical order): Bruce Anton, Shirley Bahadur, Roger Belix, Ian Brierley, Stephen Broadbridge, Andrea De Silva, Peter Hanoomansingh, Kris Rampersad, Tobago Tourism Authority, Clement Williams.

And finally, to Pamela Mary for caring so much.

Arif Ali
Port of Spain

Foreword

Minister of Tourism, Howard Chin-Lee, after launching the book Hansib published on Tobago in November 2005 at the Trinidad and Tobago High Commission in London, requested that we produce a new edition of Trinidad and Tobago – Terrific and Tranquil; the first edition was published in 2000.

The twin-island state is unique in many ways. Oil and gas drives the economy making the country the richest among the Caricom countries supported by a knowledgeable and aggressive business sector.

The 1.3 million people in Trinidad and Tobago represent every continent living together in harmony and tolerance. This year, the country celebrated the 200th anniversary of the Chinese community presence with a national holiday on 12 October. The date may now be added to the fifteen national holidays, including Independence Day, Emancipation Day and Indian Arrival Day.

The country has produced world-class writers, performers and sports people and can boast the only musical instrument to be invented in the 20th century – the steelpan. It is the birthplace of calypso and is the home of "the greatest show on Earth" – Carnival. This spectacular event has influenced similar festivals throughout the world, especially in other Caribbean countries and among Caribbean communities in Europe and North America. In Britain, the now world-famous Notting Hill Carnival has become Europe's biggest street festival. Nowhere is this vibrancy and passion more eloquently stated than in the official description of the national flag: "Red is the colour most expressive of our country. It represents the vitality of the land and its people, it is the warmth and energy of the sun, the courage and friendliness of the people; White is the sea by which these lands are bound, the cradle of our heritage, the purity of our aspirations and the equality of all men under the sun; Black represents for us the dedication of the people joined together by one strong bond. It is the colour of strength, of unity, of purpose and of the wealth of the land."

Trinidad and Tobago is a small nation whose wealth and people have a significant role to play in the progression and future stability of the Caribbean Community (Caricom).

Arif Ali, October 2006

Following their debut appearance in the 2006 World Cup Finals in Germany, the national football team, the 'Soca warriors' were treated to a heroes' welcome. The team is pictured with Prime Minister Patrick Manning, centre
Photo: Andrea De Silva

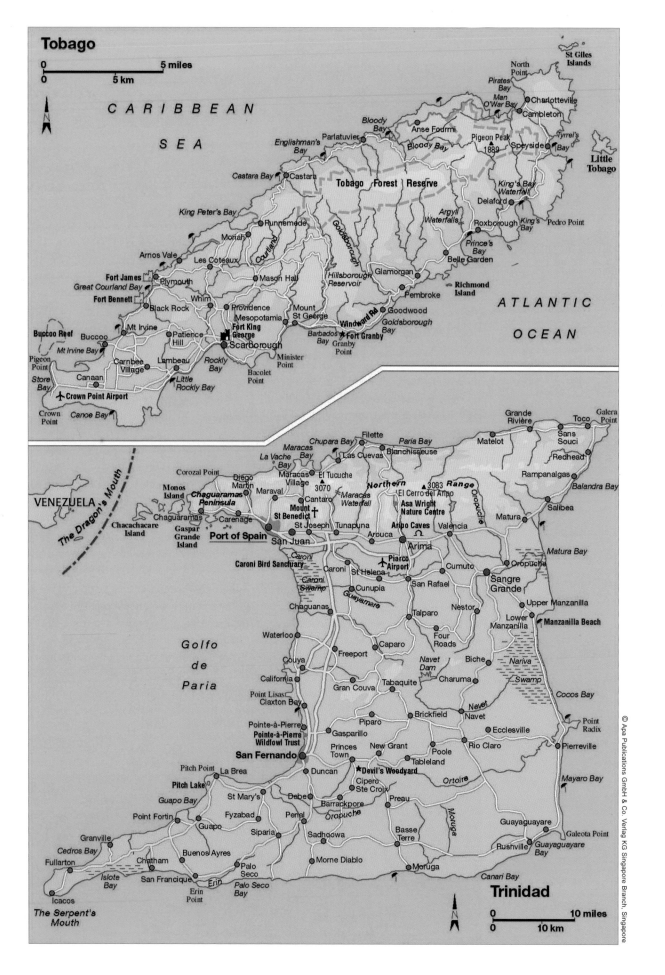

The nation in symbols

Carnival's role in national life is as overt as it is subtle. It is overt in the extended days of the Parade of the Bands, Kiddies Carnival, Panorama, fetes, calypso, soca and chutney competitions. It is subtle in the symbols that proclaim the nation – in the National Coat of Arms that seals our presence, the National Flag that we fly to claim our identity and the National Anthem that asserts our purpose in the world scheme of things.

The same vision that produces the 'Greatest Show on Earth', in fact, guided the creation of our national symbols. In the mosaic of Trinidad and Tobago, it is purely coincidental that they come from different backgrounds, different ethnicities with ancestral roots in four different continents of the world.

Two of the country's most outstanding mas (masquerade) designers, George Bailey of African ancestry along with artist Carlisle Chang, whose ancestors were of Chinese origin, are credited with designing the Coat of Arms and the National Flag. Another Carnival-influenced artiste, Pat Castagne, who composed calypso and hosted Dimanche Gras shows, composed the National Anthem.

At the dawning of the independent nation in 1962, a committee was set up to design the Flag and Coat of Arms. It included such artistic stalwarts as Carlisle Chang, George Bailey, MP Alladin, Peter Bynoe, Sybil Atteck, John Newell-Lewis and Dr John Bullbrook. A sub-committee was also established comprising of people like Tom Cambridge, Andrew Carr, Danny Samaroo, Alston Huggins, some of whom contributed to design and layout and others to choice of symbols and heritage that would be

Photo: Shirley Bahadur

THE NATIONAL ANTHEM

Forged from the Love of Liberty

Pat Castagne

Forged from the love of
liberty,
In the fires of hope and
prayer,
With boundless faith in our
Destiny,
We solemnly declare,

Side by side we stand,
Islands of the blue Caribbean
Sea,
This our Native Land,
We pledge our lives to Thee,

Here every creed and race
finds an equal place,
And may God bless our
Nation,
Here every creed and race
finds an equal place,
And may God bless our
Nation.

representative of the people of Trinidad and Tobago. The selections were approved by the College of Arms: Three colours, three birds, three hills and three ships keep

The Coat of Arms is linked to the flag of the same three colours – red, white and black. The colours represent the elements of Earth, Water and Fire, respectively. They were proclaimed by the committee to "encompass all our past, present and future and inspire us as one united, vital, free and dedicated people." The committee's official description states: "Red is the colour most expressive of our country. It represents the vitality of the land and its people; it is the warmth and energy of the sun, the courage and friendliness of the people.

"White is the sea by which these lands are bound; the cradle of our heritage; the purity of our aspirations and the equality of all men under the sun; black represents for us the dedication of the people joined together by one strong bond. It is the colour of strength, of unity, of purpose and of the wealth of the land.'

The three birds featured on the design are two from Trinidad (the scarlet ibis and the hummingbird) and from Tobago, the native cocrico. The cocrico, (rufus tailed guan) also called the Tobago pheasant, is native to Tobago and Venezuela, but is not found in Trinidad. The three ships represent the Trinity as well as the three ships of Columbus – the Santa Maria, the Pinta and the Nina with which he opened up Trinidad's gates to Europe and the rest of the world.

Retained from British colonial seals and flag badges of Trinidad were the three peaks, also representing the three peaks of the Moruga Hills which inspired Columbus to name them La Trinity and the island La Trinidad. From the British Tobago seal comes the coconut palm which sits at the top of the crest. They sit on a sea with two islands, Trinidad and Tobago, with the Motto: "Together we aspire, Together we achieve".

TRINIDAD AND TOBAGO
FACTS & FIGURES

Full name
Republic of Trinidad and Tobago

Area
5,128 sq km (1,980 sq miles)

Location
Southernmost Caribbean islands of the Lesser Antilles chain, situated between the Caribbean Sea and the North Atlantic Ocean off the northern coastline of mainland South America

Population: 1.3 million (est.)

Capital City: Port of Spain

Nationality
Trinidadian / Tobagonian

Languages
English (official language), Hindi, French, Spanish, Chinese

Religions
Roman Catholic 26%, Hindu 22.5%, Anglican 7.8%, Baptist 7.2%, Pentecostal 6.8%, other Christian 5.8%, Muslim 5.8%, Seventh Day Adventist 4%, other 10.8%, unspecified 1.4%, none 1.9% (2000 census)

Ethnic groups
East Indian 40%, African 37.5%, mixed 20.5%, other 1.2%, unspecified 0.0% (2000 census)

Literacy
98.6%

Currency
Trinidad and Tobago Dollar (TTD)

GDP per capita
Purchasing power parity   USD 18,700 (2005 est.)

Exchange Rate
USD 1 = TTD 6.3 approx.
GBP 1 = TTD 11.7 approx.

Government
Republic within the Commonwealth

Political system
Parliamentary democracy

Political parties in Parliament
People's National Movement PNM
United National Congress UNC
Congress of the People COP
Democratic Action Committee DAC (only active in Tobago)

Parties not in Parliament
National Alliance for Reconstruction or NAR
Team Unity TU

Judicial system
Supreme Court of Judicature consisting of the High Court of Justice and the Court of Appeals; High Court of Justice; Permanent Court of Appeals member; Court of Appeals; the highest court of appeal is the Privy Council in London

Legislature
Bicameral Parliament consisting of the Senate (31 seats; 16 members appointed by the ruling party, 9 by the President, 6 by the opposition party for a maximum term of five years) and the House of Representatives (41 seats; members are elected by popular vote to serve five-year terms). Tobago has a unicameral House of Assembly with 12 members serving four-year terms

Chief of State
President George Maxwell Richards (since March 2003)

Head of Government
Prime Minister Patrick Manning (since December 2001)

Main cities & towns
Port of Spain (capital)
San Fernando
Chaguanas
Arima
Point Fortin
Scarborough (Tobago)

Administrative divisions
Nine regional corporations, two city corporations, three borough corporations, one ward
Regional corporations
Couva/Tabaquite/Talparo, Diego Martin, Mayaro/Rio Claro, Penal/Debe, Princes Town, Sangre Grande, San Juan/Laventille, Siparia, Tunapuna/Piarco

Other national symbols not on the Coat of Arms are the national flower, the chaconia, also known as the wild poinsettia or 'Pride of Trinidad and Tobago'. It was named after the last Spanish Governor of Trinidad and Tobago, Don Jose Maria Chacon. Indigenous to Trinidad, it blooms in August around Independence Day.

The steelpan has been proclaimed the National Instrument of Trinidad and Tobago. Indigenous to these islands, and the only musical instrument invented in the 20th Century, it evolved out of the affluent oil industry of the country, on one hand, and the creative industry of some of the most disadvantaged. The oil industry provided the steel drums on which was pounded out the notes that produce the percussion sounds of steel.

Carlisle Chang (1921–2001)

Carlisle Chang paved the way for the work of local artists to be considered seriously as a means to a livelihood, achieved largely because of his versatility in sculpting, painting, costume designing, set designing, teaching, and a designer of Carnival bands. His achievements came with high cost to himself, including the pain of seeing his most acclaimed work, 'The Inherent Nobility of Man', a mural which lay on the walls of the Piarco International Airport, torn down to make way for expansion in 1981. His 'Conquerabia', named after one of his earlier incarnations of the capital city, is cast in concrete on the walls of City Hall in Port of Spain.

City corporations
Port of Spain, San Fernando
Borough corporations
Arima, Chaguanas, Point Fortin
Ward: Tobago

Independence
31 August 1962 (from Great Britain)

Membership of international organisations
Caribbean Community and Common Market (CARICOM), Caribbean Development Bank (CDB), Group of 24, Association of Caribbean States (ACS), Food and Agricultural Organisation (FAO), Group of 77, Group of African Caribbean and Pacific (ACP) countries, Inter-American Development Bank (IDB), International Monetary Fund (IMF), International Labour Organisation (ILO), Interpol, IOC, ISO, International Telecommunications Union (ITU), Organization of American States (OAS), UNCTAD, UNESCO, UNIDO, United Nations (UN), WHO, World Intellectual Property Organization (WIPO), World Trade Organisation (WTO)

Trade agreements
Caricom Single Market, Caricom/Domincan Republic, Caricom/Costa Rica, Caricom/Cuba, European Union/African Caribbean Pacific agreements (last being Cotonou, now being negotiated for what will be known as Economic Partnership Agreements)

Preferential Trade Arrangements
Caribbean Basin Trade Partnership Act - with the US, Caribcan (with Canada)

Double Taxation Treaties
Canada, France, Denmark, Germany, Italy, Norway, Switzerland, United Kingdom, Venezuela, United States, Caricom and currently negotiating with Spain

National Flower: Chaconia

National Bird
Scarlet Ibis (Trinidad), Cocrico (Tobago)

National Motto
Together We Aspire Together We Achieve

National holidays & celebrations

January 1	New Year's Day
February-March	† Carnival Monday
	† Carnival Tuesday
March 30	Spiritual Baptist Shouters Liberation Day
April	†† Good Friday
	†† Easter Sunday
	†† Easter Monday
May 30	Indian Arrival Day
June 10	Corpus Christi
June 19	Labour Day
August 1	Emancipation Day
August 31	Independence Day
September 24	Republic Day
October 12	Chinese Arrival Day (2006)
October-November	* Divali
October-November	** Eid-ul-Fitr
December 25	Christmas Day
December 26	Boxing Day

NOTE: Date variations
† Carnival Monday and Tuesday precede Ash Wednesday
†† Good Friday and Easter holidays come at end of Lent
* Divali is a religious holiday and depends on moon phase – darkest night
** Eid is a religious holiday and depends on new moon sighting

Climate
Tropical; rainy season June to December

Time zone
GMT minus 4 hours

Natural resources
Petroleum, Natural Gas, Asphalt (Pitch Lake on the south-western coast, is the world's largest natural reservoir of asphalt), Eco Tourism

Highest point
El Cerro del Aripo 940 m

Main river
Caroni

Internet country code: .tt

Telephone dialling code: 868

George Bailey (1935-1970)

Unlike Carlisle Chang, George Bailey both designed and owned a Carnival band. In 1957 (aged only twenty-two), he produced the band, 'Back To Africa', a band that celebrated the spirit of the continent rather than lament over it deprivation. It took that year's Band of the Year title. It was clearly the idiom for which Carnival was searching, asserting its place in the world in finding affinity with cultures of the world. Bailey followed this with another win in 1959 with the band, 'Relic of Egypt', taking not just the Band of the Year title but also the People's Choice Award. It was the beginning of four successive wins for Bailey. He died when he was only 35.

Pat Castagne (1916-2000)

The music of Christmas and Carnival owe almost as much to Pat Castagne, as does the National Anthem. Castagne was, in fact, a writer, producer and host of the grand Carnival Sunday show – Dimanche Gras – when he was chosen to write the 1962 National Anthem for Trinidad and Tobago's Independence Day celebrations. It was originally called 'A Song for the Islands', written for the West Indies Federation, but when the Federation collapsed, he presented the song to Trinidad and Tobago. One line of the submission to the Federation, "hands joined across the sea", was rewritten as "islands of the blue Caribbean Sea." ∎

Photo: Stephen Broadbridge

A unique Caribbean experience

In a region renowned for its natural beauty and diverse culture, the twin-island republic of Trinidad and Tobago (5,128 sq km) remains utterly unique. Unlike the volcanic or limestone and coral formations to the north, these southernmost outposts of the Lesser Antilles island chain share a common geology with the South American mainland to which they were once joined. Trinidad's Northern Range is the true end of the Andes and this South American past accounts for the flora and fauna of both islands, which is unsurpassed in diversity and quantity by any other Caribbean island.

But Trinidad and Tobago's uniqueness is not limited to its natural resources, which include Trinidad's Pitch Lake and Tobago's Central Forest Reserve – the oldest protected rainforest in the Western Hemisphere. History has conspired, largely unwittingly, to create in Trinidad one of the world's most cosmopolitan societies and multi-ethnic cultures, while in Tobago, one of the Caribbean's strongest African cultures survives proudly in the age of the Internet.

Originally settled by Amerindian tribes from the north-west shoulder of South America, who called it "Iere" (land of the hummingbird), Trinidad owes its modern name to Columbus, who sighted three hills off the southern coast in 1498. Tobago retains the Amerindian name for tobacco, a reminder of one of the European obsessions which, like gold and then sugar, would dominate the history of the islands during the colonial era.

While the Dutch, Latvians, French and English fought over Tobago in a bid to realise the dream of becoming "as rich as a Tobago planter", Trinidad languished as a backwater of Spain's colonial empire until the late 18th century. The Spanish crown's call for Roman Catholic settlers resulted in an influx of French planters and their African slaves from Martinique, Grenada and Haiti.

This was the beginning of modern Trinidad. The French cleared the forests for plantations, introduced carnival and Creole joie de vivre, which would become the bedrock of 'Trini' culture when allied with that of the slaves. When the British arrived in 1797, they found themselves ruling a colony of French Creole speakers governed by Spanish law. After full Emancipation in 1838, the Trini spice just got nicer: indentured labourers imported from China, India and Madeira; African slaves liberated at sea by the British navy; and Middle Eastern hucksters all joined in the evolution of one of the most mixed, creative and harmonious societies on the planet. Here, Christian, Hindu and Muslim live side-by-side, giving real meaning to the 'Trinbagonian' claim that, "All of we is one".

Carnival, calypso and steelpan are just some of the unique expressions of this society; achievements out of all proportion to its actual size. Referred to locally as a 'callaloo' (a rich soup of distinctive ingredients), Trinidad's multi-ethnic culture is instantly apparent in its inventive use of language, its architecture (from the 'Magnificent Seven' of the Queen's Park Savannah to the mandirs and mosques located throughout the country), and its cuisine, which draws on African, Indian and Chinese heritage.

Trinidad, like its smaller sister island, is surely blessed. South of the devastating hurricane belt, this safe haven enjoys energy resources (oil, natural gas and associated

ABOVE: Cathedral of the Immaculate Conception in Independence Square in Port of Spain

Photo: Shirley Bahadur

Photo: Bruce Anton

petrochemicals) which have made it the financial, commercial and industrial centre of the Eastern Caribbean, as well as the undisputed party capital of the region. The nation's capital, Port of Spain, combines a colonial past with all the amenities and lifestyle of a 21st century metropolis. Modern landmarks like the new National Library complex and the skyscrapers which line the Brian Lara Promenade on Independence Square, complement the old style of the Red House parliament building and the intricate fretwork of the wooden gingerbread houses of the suburbs. Along the seashore of the western peninsula, drive-in shopping malls, condominiums and luxury apartment blocks are all manifestations of Trinidad's willingness to embrace the future.

But one of the many paradoxes of Trinidad is that only a short drive from the bustling capital, one can stray into the past of rural Indian villages, where Hindu prayer flags flutter in the breeze and ox-drawn carts loaded with sugarcane are as familiar sights as a caiman waddling along the road.

San Fernando, in the south, is Trinidad's second city and owes much of its importance to the proximity of the oilfields both on land and at sea. Chaguanas, on the central plain, is probably the island's fastest growing urban centre, while Point Fortin is another oil belt settlement and Arima, in the east, is an old cocoa town whose Santa Rosa district is home to the descendants of the island's original Carib inhabitants.

Out of the republic's total population of 1.3 million, there are only 50,000 Tobagonians, mostly of African descent. African folklore and the African rhythms of

ABOVE: Overlooking St Andrews Golf Club in the Maraval Valley

FACING PAGE
Maracas Beach

Photos: Ian Brierley

tambrin music survive in hilltop villages like Moriah and Whim and are showcased in the annual Heritage Festival. Scarborough is the only town of any size and the 'Tranquil Isle' is justifiably proud of its much slower lifestyle. Party in Trinidad and chill out in Tobago is good advice for any visitor. With its pristine beaches and the best dive sites in the Eastern Caribbean, Tobago has developed a niche market for sustainable eco-tourism, in contrast to islands with gated, all-inclusive resorts and mass arrivals.

Trinidad's carnival may have put it on the world map but more recently Trinidad and Tobago has graced the world stage with its football team, the Soca Warriors, who gave such a spirited performance at the 2006 World Cup finals in Germany. Team captain, Tobagonian Dwight Yorke and Trinidadian Russell Latapy were both veterans of the 1989 team and are among the first of an increasing number of local footballers who now play professionally in Europe, America, Japan and Australia.

But if football is high profile, then cricket is like food, drink and carnival itself to 'Trinbagonians'. The record-breaking batsman, Brian Lara is a twin-island hero who began his career on a village pitch in Cantaro. Sport features as prominently as music and partying in Trinidad and Tobago's lifestyle, whether it's a heated card game of 'all fours' in the rum shop, or World Cup cricket at the Queen's Park Oval. If you're looking for terrific action and tranquil relaxation, with the past alive in the present, and a totally unique Caribbean experience, you will find it all in Trinidad and Tobago. ■

ABOVE: Canoe
bay in Tobago
Photo: P Hanoomansingh

RIGHT: Roman
Catholic church in
St Joseph
Photo: S Broadbridge

FACING PAGE
Mandir in San
Fernando

ABOVE: Laventille
Photo: Shirley Bahadur

Photo: Stephen Broadbridge

FACING PAGE
The statue of the Hindu god, Hanuman,
is located in Waterloo

Yachts moored in
Chaguaramas
Photo: B Anton

OVERLEAF
Yellow, or golden
poui tree, left, at
the Queen's Park
Savannah in Port
of Spain; and,
right, the Jinnah
Mosque in St
Joseph

A UNIQUE CARIBBEAN EXPERIENCE

ABOVE: Mount Pleasant Village
Photo: Bruce Anton

RIGHT: Stollmeyer's Castle is one
of the 'Magnificent Seven' buildings
situated around the Queen's Park
Savannah in Port of Spain
Photo: Shirley Bahadur

FACING PAGE
The Blue Grotto is located in the
Gasparee Caves which were once
used by pirates and smugglers

PREVIOUS PAGES
Maracas Beach

Wider view of history

Most accounts of the history of Trinidad and Tobago begin with the sighting of land by Christopher Columbus during his third voyage to the region in 1498. But a longer view of the islands' past – that is less Eurocentric – can extend the history of these islands to several more centuries and even many more epochs than have traditionally been acknowledged.

To delve deeper into the history of the islands, even before human settlement, geological evidence points to a time when Trinidad was part of the South American continent, until tectonic plate collision forced a separation. Some rocks within the folds of the Northern Range, for instance, date to the late Jurassic period, distinguishing the island from others in the Caribbean archipelago which largely formed from sedimentation during the Miocene period.

An ecological perspective endorses this long history of the islands in the varieties of species of flora and fauna that establishes ties with the continent. One example is the scarlet ibis that make their homes between South America and Trinidad.

The year 1498 signalled the beginning of the recorded history of the islands, but the human history began thousands of years earlier.

Banwari Man, the oldest human fossils found on the island (and in the Caribbean region), places human habitation of Trinidad to at least 7000 BC, just about the time when the island was separated from the South American mainland. What occurred in human habitation between 7000 BC and 1492 remains buried in the unrecorded annals of prehistory. It is nevertheless firmly established from remnants of settlements unearthed in Blanchisseuse, Moruga, Mayaro and San Francique, for example, that the descendants of Banwari Man had established a remarkable civilization through nomadic to settled existence. They relied on hunting, fishing and later agriculture for survival, with their own social, political and economic structures and systems, that even involved trade, exchange and interaction with other islands and other settlements on the neighbouring South American continent.

Arguably, the first peoples (who called Trinidad 'Kairi') carried the oral history of the island's separation from the continent, if one is to take their naming of rivers both in South America and Trinidad as River Caroni, as an example.

This debunks the historical repetition that Domingo de Vera established the first settlement in San Jose De Oruna (St Joseph) in 1592, though he might still lay claim to having established the first settlement in the name of Spain after failed attempts by the Spanish to settle in 1531. It follows in the history books that Sir Walter Raleigh would sail into this town, up the Caroni River after caulking leaks in his ship at the Pitch Lake (which itself has a history that dates back to another epoch) and destroy the Spanish capital in the name of Queen Elizabeth. The Spanish would effect virtual genocide of the native population, through its system of 'encomienda' which attempted to contain them within four districts that still bear names in the native language – Tacarigua, Arima, Arouca.

The invitation, in 1783, to French settlers from other islands to populate Trinidad, added to the European mix.

All of the systems and institutions of the first peoples of the islands have given way to those of the new inhabitants, the Spanish. But after nearly 200 years of occupation, the Spanish were run out by the British in 1797 without much of a skirmish. In its less than 200 years of dominance, Britain introduced what would be the foundation of most of the country's institutions – in law, politics, education and other social system, through the succession of Governors she sent in to rule.

Britain's slave trade brought in new populations of Africans to work sugar, cocoa and coffee estates, until the practice was ended in 1807 followed by the emancipation edict which was passed in 1834 and came into effect in 1838. African slave labour was the largest group of forced immigration that occurred through the slave trade until its abolition.

Britain needed a new workforce and it turned to Asia – first with indentured Chinese, Syrian and

Lebanese labour, before drawing from the vast population of India in 1845 until indentured immigration ceased in 1917. Britain was already losing interests in her colonies as sources of wealth in the waning of their sugar, cocoa and tobacco industries. One symptom of this was her warding Tobago to Trinidad in 1899.

In the next half a century, the newly-introduced groups, with those of European descent, would establish the roots of modern Trinidad and Tobago. Together, Africans, Indians and Europeans, inspired by the independence movement in India, would collaborate for labour rights and lobby for independence from Britain, which came in 1962.

The independent twin-island state would, however, continue to keep institutions laid down by Britain, including its system of Parliamentary Democracy that has a Prime Minister and a Cabinet as the executive head; a legislative arm in two houses of Parliament – one elected and the other appointed; and a judicial arm. Replacement of the British-appointed Governor with a President who holds only residual and ceremonial powers would come in 1976, with the declaration of the Republic of Trinidad and Tobago.

Now, just about half a century since Britain relinquished control, her inherited systems are being challenged to meet the demands of an evolving society that is now moving under its own steam, though in directions often dictated by new world powers. The Constitution, largely adopted from the British, is under pressure to accommodate new realities and is now under review. Similar demands are being made on institutions of law and order, education, social systems and even media.

The national holidays of Trinidad and Tobago, largely, reflect the presence of the various migrant groups within the country. By the twists that are sometimes evident in a long view of history, July 31, once celebrated as Discovery Day and which should mark the European presence on the island, was removed from the national calendar. There is no holiday to recognise the native peoples. A parade of a statue through the streets of Arima known as the festival of Santa Rosa – an ironic collaboration between the Catholic Church and the descendants of native peoples – is an annual reminder of their existence. But there are holidays to mark Liberation Day on March 30 in remembrance of the revocation of the Prohibition Ordinance that prevented Spiritual Baptists from practicing their religion; Emancipation Day on August 1, Arrival Day to mark the coming of the Indians on May 30 and most recently, Chinese Arrival Day celebrated on October 12 for the first time in 2006. The secular holidays are New Year's Day on January 1, Labour Day on June 19 marking the labour riots that preceded the drive to Independence; Independence Day on August 31; Republic Day on September 24 marking replacement of the Queen as the ceremonial head of state with a local President.

The other holidays are related to religious festivities of the multicultural society – Divali for the Hindus, Eid for Muslims, and for Christians, Corpus Christi on June 15, Christmas and Boxing Days and Good Friday to Easter. The pre-Lenten Carnival festivities that culminate in the two-day Parade of the Bands on the Monday and Tuesday before Ash Wednesday and the beginning of Lent are not official holidays but are treated as such by most of the population.

The ability of nature to redirect the course of human, and economic history has made its mark time and again. The tectonic upheavals that caused separation from the mainland would have been one of those. Less dramatic, but significant nonetheless, was the witchbroom disease of 1928 that swept the cocoa plantations and re-coursed the island's economy from one built upon cocoa and sugar cane production, to one that relied solely upon sugar cane. Cane was king until petroleum gradually overtook the economy of Trinidad from the 1930s. Now, in the new millennium, natural gas is the rising star. In a similar vein, when Hurricane Flora swept through Tobago in 1963, it changed the island's economic focus from a largely agricultural base to one that is largely fuelled by tourism.

Photo: Shirley Bahadur

A rich blend of cultural influences

SIMON LEE

Where on earth would you find African drummers participating in a festival, which has sacred Shi'ite Muslim roots; grown men betting seriously on a goat race, or Hindus worshipping a Black Virgin at a Roman Catholic shrine? Again, where could you witness the astonishing pre-dawn spectacle of men and women smeared top to toe in dripping blue paint, waving wire tails and pitchforks menacingly at anyone foolish enough to be on the streets at this ungodly hour? Which land on Earth gives itself over wholeheartedly to the serious business of partying from Boxing Day night right through to dusk on Shrove Tuesday and then heads for mass on Ash Wednesday morning? These examples are only some of the many expressions of Trinidad and Tobago's ever-surprising culture.

But then in Trinidad and Tobago, always expect the unexpected, for this is a nation of two separate territories, many different ethnic groups and religions, and discrete and common cultures. You'd be hard pressed to find a population as ethnically or culturally mixed as Trinidad's, in such a small place, anywhere else in the world.

Here you'll encounter Amerindians, Europeans, Africans, Asians, Cocoa Payols (descendants of Black peons from Venezuela), Arabs, Chinese and every possible combination derived from the mixing of these parent communities. While in Tobago, the majority are of African descent. And it is this melange which holds the key to Trinidad and Tobago's culture.

Take the language first. There are immediate clues to this multi-heritage in the place names: Amerindian – Naparima, Chacachacare, Guayaguayare; Spanish – Palo Seco, Sangre Grande, San Rafael; French – Bourg Mulatresse, Champs Fleur, Lopinot; and English – Scarborough, Plymouth, Princes Town. If Trinis are discussing the weather they might say, "It making hot", a French construction as in "Il fait chaud". Linguistic anachronisms like this are survivors from the 19th century when Trinidad's lingua franca was French Creole.

Nowadays, the official language is English, but Trinidadian English Creole is spoken by all. And those expecting to hear standard English will be surprised at nouns serving as verbs (to "advantage someone" or "to expense yourself"), and local idioms whose origins are the guesswork of linguists: 'basodee' and 'tootolbey'. You'll meet 'maccos' and 'mampies' but it's best not to give them a 'cut eye'. But 'in truth and in fact', 'jump high, jump low', the most relevant word to Trinbagonian culture is 'liming', which has nothing to do with citrus fruit but refers to that quintessential Trini activity of hanging out, chilling, relaxing among friends or acquaintances.

While Tobago's Creole is thought to share more in common with Jamaica's (due to common African roots), both islands have a fund of distinctive folk proverbs. If a Trini tells you "Crapaud smoke yuh pipe", you're in imminent trouble, but then you can take comfort in the Tobagonian reassurance, "Jackass say world nuh level" – life just ain't fair. From the same African-Creole source comes such folklore figures as Papa Bois, guardian of the forest, Mama Glo, spirit of the rivers, La Diablesse, the fatally attractive cloven-hoofed temptress, the Lagahou, which feeds on blood and can change shape along with its female counterpart the Soucouyant, who sheds her wrinkled old skin at

Spiritual Baptists
in San Fernando
Photo: S Broadbridge

ABOVE: 'Liming' at Maracas Beach
Photo: Shirley Bahadur

nights to travel as a ball of fire in search of victims, and the male mermaids of Tobago.

Again it is the diversity of peoples which accounts for the range of religions in Trinidad and Tobago. The Spanish and then the French brought Roman Catholicism with them and the original Cathedral of the Immaculate Conception on Independence Square in Port of Spain dates from 1781. Catholics make up nearly thirty percent of the population closely followed by Hindus, Anglicans (who arrived with the British), Muslims, Presbyterians and smaller numbers of Moravians, Seventh Day Adventists. There are many Pentecostal sects and adherents of Trinidad's indigenous Shouter or Spiritual Baptist African-Christian syncretic religion and the Yoruban Orisha or Shango faith brought by slaves from West Africa. Small but significant minorities are the Bobo Shantis, who practise a fusion of Ethiopian Christianity, Garveyism and Judaism, and Rastafarians and Kali worshippers. Between the realms of formal religion and folklore, Obeah, the West African practice of magic, is closely allied with bush medicine or herbal healing.

With so many religions comes Trinidad and Tobago's exceptional number of fourteen public holidays. Christmas is celebrated by all regardless of faith and has acquired a distinctive celebratory character due to its association with the carnival season of slavery

TOP RIGHT: Santa Rosa parade in Arima
Photo: Roger Belix

RIGHT: Phagwa celebrations
Photo: Andrea De Silva

days, complete with its own seasonal music, Spanish-derived parang. Easter (with its beating of the 'bobolee', originally a stuffed effigy of Judas)) and Corpus Christi, are also major events, as is Siparia's entirely indigenous La Divina Pastora festival, celebrated on the second Sunday after Easter. A wooden statue of the Black Virgin is paraded through the streets, worshipped by both Catholics and Hindus who know it as Soparee Kay Mai, or Kali, destroyer of sorrow.

Hindu and Muslim festivals have become an integral part of the cultural calendar. Phagwa, March's Hindu spring festival is celebrated on savannahs throughout the island to the singing of chowtal or pichakaaree songs and the drenching of all with colourful abeer. Divali, the November Hindu festival of lights, is now celebrated on both islands. In the preceding weeks, besides numerous lighting-up events, when thousands of small clay deyas filled with oil and wicks are lit, the Hindu epic of Ram and Sita, the 'Ramleela', is enacted at dusk by village troupes to the commentary of pandits. Divali night itself is a magical twinkling of millions of deyas and Hindus distribute bags of prasad (containing deep-fried sweetened dough or kurma, raisins and slices of apple or banana) to family, friends and neighbours.

ABOVE & RIGHT: Phagwa celebrations
Photo: Andrea De Silva

BELOW: Lighting deyas in preparation
for Divali
Photo: Peter Hanoomansingh

FACING PAGE
Celebrating the Hindu festival of Divali
Photo: Andrea De Silva

ABOVE: Tambrin drummers at a Moriah
wedding during the Tobago Festival
Photo: Clement Williams

FACING PAGE
Carnival is Trinidad's gift to the world
Photo: Stephen Broadbridge

Eid-ul Fitr, the end of the Islamic fasting month of Ramadan, is eagerly anticipated by all, for the delicious sweet rice or sawaine. Hosay, celebrated at the end of the month of Muharram and which originated in a sacred Shi'ite Muslim festival commemorating the martyrdom of the prophet Mohammed's grandsons, Hassan and Husein, has taken on all the colour, creative and musical energy of carnival, with the parading of tadjahs (elaborate replicas of the martyrs' tombs), the moon dance and beating of tassa drums.

But the major festival which unites all races, religions and the whole social spectrum is Trinidad's gift to the world: carnival, which has developed over two hundred years as a totally unique expression of Creole culture. Calypso and soca, steelpan, stickfighting and elaborately costumed masquerade bands are all part of 'the greatest show on earth'.

Carnival changes with the times. Originally exclusive to the French planters who introduced it and who held formal masked balls and house parties, it became the people's festival after full Emancipation in 1838. The Jamette carnival (named after the 'diametre' or urban under class) was a celebration of freedom, excess and wildness; a time for the ex-slaves to beat their drums, sing their songs, mock their former masters and, in the process, affront the respectability of both the colonial authorities and the emerging Black bourgeoisie.

After the African drum, the torchlight procession of Canboulay and masking were all banned in the 1880s, the lewder and more violent aspects of the festival were gradually exorcised and it began its transition into the more sanitised and commercialised form of today. Viey Lakou provides an insight into old time carnival and its traditional characters (Midnight Robber, Dame Lorraine, Burrokeet, Pierrot Grenade), while the wild spirit of excess lives on in the spontaneity of Jouvert.

While carnival claims most of Trinidad's creative energy, October's Best Village competition ensures the survival of folk arts and crafts. Villages and towns compete

Drummers
celebrating the
festival of Hosay
Photo: Shirley Bahadur

CHINESE ARRIVAL DAY

To mark the 200th anniversary of the arrival of the Chinese community in Trinidad and Tobago (1807-2006), the date of 12 October was officially designated as a public holiday in 2006

using traditional dances, songs and storytelling to present their themes. The African-derived kalenda, limbo, bongo and saraka are danced along with the Creole bele and pique, with the women wearing the national dress of full bele skirt and brightly-coloured head tie, and the men in white shirt, black trousers and coloured sash. Tobago's Heritage Festival in July preserves the sister isle's own unique culture, while the Easter Tuesday goat and crab races at Buccoo are attended by islanders and bemused visitors in their thousands.

To truly sample Trinidad and Tobago's culture, an ideal place to begin is the cuisine – as varied as the callaloo soup which has become emblematic of the nation's cosmopolitan society. All cultures are represented on the national menu, which utilises seasoning from the various heritages to produce a unique flavour: Amerindian fiery pepper, coriander, geera, curry (introduced by East Indians) and a whole range of locally-grown herbs and spices.

Cassava, an Amerindian staple, provides bakes and bread and roasted corn is another favourite snack from the pre-Columbian era. The Spanish legacy lives on in the pastelles of Christmas (cornmeal wraps filled with beef or pork, raisins and olives), escoviche, buljol (saltfish, tomato, lime, pepper garlic and avocado). French Creole cuisine – a mixture of African dishes and recipes introduced by the French planters – serves up the callaloo, pelau (rice, pigeon peas and chicken) and coocoo, along with the 'blue food' or ground provisions (mostly tubers like cassava, yam, dasheen, eddoes) the former slaves would grow on their small plots to supplement their diet.

ABOVE: Roast corn is available from many roadside sellers

RIGHT: The popular 'bake and shark'

BOTTOM: Christmas in Trinidad and Tobago is not complete without black cake

FACING PAGE
The ubiquitous, home-made pepper sauce and chutney
Photos: Shirley Bahadur

PREVIOUS PAGE
Dancing the 'brush-back' during the Tobago Festival
Photo: Tobago Tourism Authority

Indian cuisine is as popular as Creole: curries (particularly the famous curried duck seasoned with fiery Scotch bonnet pepper, obligatory fare at any river lime), roti (dough wraps filled with meat, seafood or vegetables and seasoned with pepper and spicy mango chutney) and Trinidad and Tobago's cheapest and most popular fast food, doubles (a wrap of 'barra' dough containing highly seasoned channa or chickpeas), can all be considered national dishes. Indian sweetmeats and delicacies (jelibi, ladoo) and snacks (phoulorie, aloo pie, katchowrie) are on roadside offer along with fresh coconuts (the juice is a tested stomach settler) and fruit, and a variety of drinks like seamoss and peanut punch, recommended for energy and fertility.

The Chinese community has developed its own Trini-style of cooking and the chow mein is highly regarded along with pepper shrimp. Potato salad, a must-have with barbecue or Sunday lunch, is a Lebanese contribution.

Christmas has its own special dishes and drinks: pork and ham, black cake (preserved fruit soaked in rum for months), sorrel, ginger beer and ponche a crème (a rum egg nog). Throughout the year fresh fruit juice (soursop, barbadine, mango, grapefruit, lime) is a popular refreshment while the rumshops cater for those who like their rum, 'beastly cold beers' and a lime which anyone is always welcome to join.

Trinbagonians love their food as much as their country and eating and drinking with them is a delicious introduction to their culture. Bon appetit, or, "eat good" as we say. ■

Photo: Shirley Bahadur

The greatest show on Earth

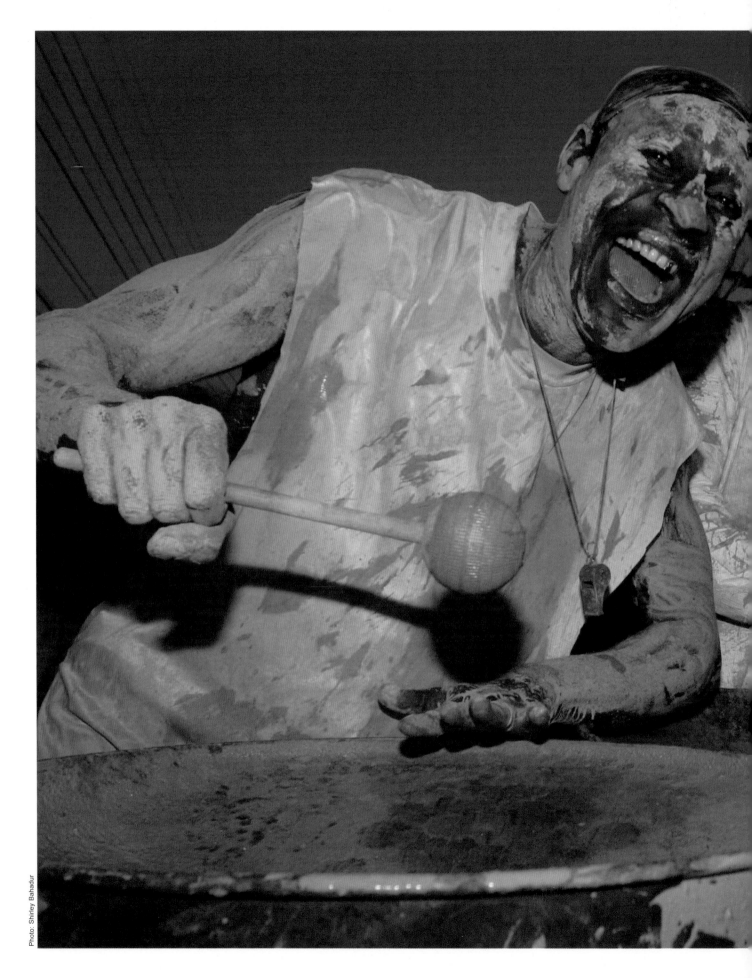

Photo: Shirley Bahadur

Steelpan – the sound of Trinidad and Tobago

Photo: Andrea De Silva

Photo: Shirley Bahadur

Photo: Shirley Bahadur

Photo: Stephen Broadbridge

Photo: Stephen Broadbridge

Photo: Andrea De Silva

Heroes' welcome for the Soca Warriors

PHOTOS: ANDREA DE SILVA

The faces of Trinidad and Tobago

Photo: Andrea De Silva

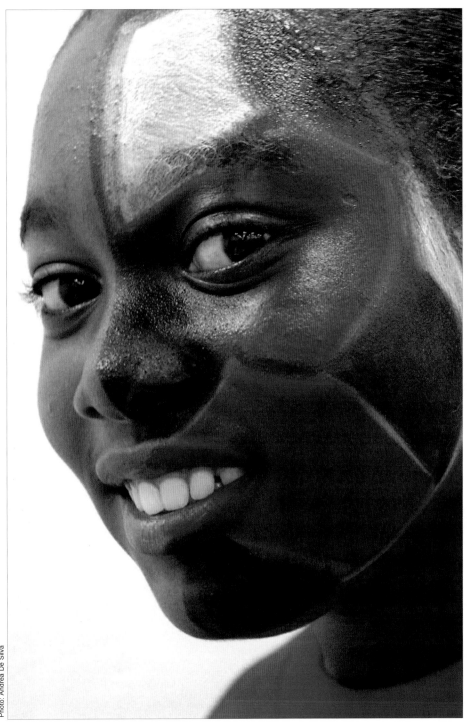

Photo: Andrea De Silva

Photo: Shirley Bahadur

Photo: Ian Brierley

Photo: Shirley Bahadur

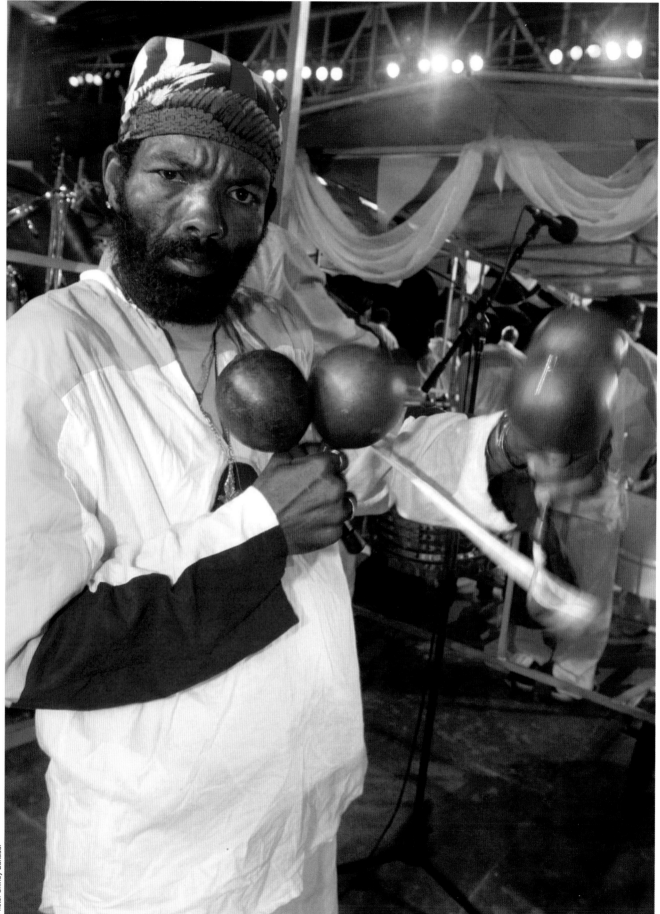

Photo: Shirley Bahadur

A fusion of forms

SIMON LEE

Given Trinidad and Tobago's natural mixing abilities, it's not surprising to find fusion forms like parang soca and chutney soca, or jazz and world musicians like calypso jazz pioneer Zanda, world-acclaimed jazz guitarist Fitzroy Coleman, the late Andre Tanker, who played all Caribbean styles to native Orisha-inspired rhythms, and Indo-calypso jazz improviser Mungal Patasar, whose combination of pan and sitar epitomises Trini musical heritage.

Trinidad and Tobago's rich African rhythmic roots have been the fruitful ground for the development of both calypso ('the people's newspaper') and steelpan, the only acoustic instrument invented in the twentieth century.

The Indian presence since 1845 has had a profound influence on Trinidad's sound-scape. The tassa drum, originally introduced as accompaniment to the Muslim Hosay festival, has become a regular feature of percussion. Classical Indian and film singing, the chowtal and pichakaree songs of Phagwa and the spicy lyrics and dancing of chutney (a fusion of Bhojpuri folksongs and the female Maticor wedding ritual) can be witnessed island-wide.

The Spanish legacy lives on in the parang music of Christmas, when aguinaldos and serenales (carols), along with lively joropos, manzanares and guarapos are sung (in distinctive Trini Spanish) to the accompaniment of cuatro, guitar, box bass and shac shac. Tobago can boast its own indigenous tambrin (shallow drum) folk form, in which African rhythms and violin accompany reel and jig dances for the ancestors, or Creole songs (sea shanties, play songs, hymns, stories).

Calypso base

Derived from the African griot tradition, a wide range of West African songs – work, story-telling, praise, mockery, topical and social commentary, and influenced by European forms and instrumentation, Kaiso, as traditional calypso is still referred to, evolved from the songs of the plantation chantwells (master singers). The earliest documented calypso, sung by the chantwell Gros Jean in praise of his satanic master, Begorrat, dates from the 1820s and by the end of nineteenth century, the first calypsos in English, rather than French Creole, could be heard.

The era between the two world wars established calypso as a classic indigenous song form, with legendary exponents like Chieftain Douglas, King Radio, Atilla the Hun, the Lords Executor and Invader and the Roaring Lion. The presence of entertainment-hungry American troops during the Second World War boosted calypso's popularity at home and abroad and gave us Invader's 'Rum and Coca Cola' commentary on the situation: "both mother and daughter, working for the Yankee dollar".

Figures like Lord Kitchener, Spoiler and Mighty Sparrow developed classic calypso's rich veins of humour, double entendre, story-telling and surrealism before the explosion of funk and soul-influenced soca in the 1970s introduced the faster-paced party style of the modern era. Shadow and Lord Shorty were the innovators of a genre, expanded by

Calypsonians, David Rudder (above) and Machel Montano

Photos: Shirley Bahadur

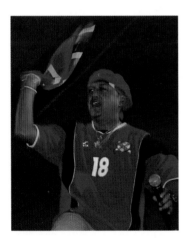

Chutney-soca star, Rikki Jai

David Rudder in the late 1980s and 90s and now dominated by such young-bloods as Machel Montano, Bunji Garlin and Maximus Dan. Rapso is another recent genre to emerge from the African oral and chanting tradition, with innovative groups like Three Canal or individuals like Ataklan, fusing indigenous elements with trans-national influences from hip-hop and ambient grooves, to dancehall and drum and bass.

Literary excellence

With their mixed linguistic heritage, Trinis have a predilection for words, spoken or written, and a literary tradition which can boast one island-born Nobel literature laureate, Sir Vidia Naipaul (2001) and strong connections with another, Derek Walcott (1992) who, although born in St Lucia, lived in Trinidad from the 1950s through to the late 70s and established the Trinidad Theatre Workshop.

Written in 1854 by Maxwell Phillips, Trinidad's first Black Solicitor General, *Emmanuel Appadocca* is regarded by some as the first Anglophone Caribbean novel. Phillips's contemporary, the brilliant, self-taught linguist and scholar, John Jacob Thomas produced his *Theory and Practice of Creole Grammar* in 1869, followed by *Froudacity* in 1889, a response to the racism of Oxford professor, James Anthony Froude's *The English in the West Indies*.

The Beacon group of the 1930s, a loose confederation of intellectuals, politicians and writers, established Trinidad and Tobago's literary tradition. Among them was C.L.R. James – "the Black Plato of the twentieth century" whose *The Black Jacobins* account of the Haitian Revolution, initiated Caribbean historiography and whose *Beyond A Boundary* remains the best ever book on cricket and Caribbean sensibility. Alfred Mendes and Ralph de Boissiere wrote 'yard novels' using social realism to foreground the lives of the urban working class and began the exploration of Trini identity which would preoccupy the work of the next generation.

Sam Selvon and V.S. Naipaul both established themselves and their writing careers in London during the 1950s. Selvon's, *The Lonely Londoners* is famous both for its humour and as the first text to use Trini vernacular rather than Standard English, while Naipaul's early work, particularly *Miguel Street* and *A House for Mr Biswas*, made great literature of Indo-Creole sensibility and lifestyle. Vidia's younger brother, Shiva, also produced some fine novels (*Fireflies*, *The Chip Chip Gatherers*) and travel writing before his early death. Other notable Indo-Trinidadian novelists-in-exile of this period include Harold Sonny Ladoo with *No Pain Like This Body* and *Yesterdays*, and Ismith Khan with *The Jumbie Bird*, among others.

Since Independence, some writers have made the unenviable attempt to forge on-island literary careers. Outstanding among these is Earl Lovelace, whose novel, *Salt*, won a Commonwealth Writer's Prize (1996-7). This work, like his earlier novels, *The Dragon Can't Dance* and *The Wine of Astonishment*, explores the complexities of the Trini Creole experience and the historical struggle to validate its own culture. Other stay-at-homes include Merle Hodge with *Crick Crack Monkey*, Valerie Belgrave's *Ti Marie*, Sharlow Mohammed and, most recently, journalist, essayist and novelist, Kevin Baldeosingh.

Many Trini novelists now flourish in the diasporas: Miami-based Robert Antoni who won a Commonwealth Writer's Prize (1992-3) for *Divina Trace*; US-based Kelvin Christopher James and Canada-based Neil Bissoondath, Dionne Brand, Claire Harris and Rabindranath Maharaj. Lawrence Scott, who teaches in London, also won a Commonwealth Writer's Prize for his 1999 novel, *Aelred*.

Beside the major figure of V.S. Naipaul, Trinidad and Tobago continues to produce gifted poets and playwrights. The tortured Tobagonian, Eric Roach walked into the sea in 1970, while Jamaica-based Trini, Wayne Browne won the 1972 Commonwealth Poetry Prize for his *On the Coast* anthology. Among the new generation Jennifer Rahim and Raymond Ramcharitar are producing work which is attracting international attention.

ABOVE & RIGHT
The ninth Carifesta celebrations were held in Trinidad and Tobago in 2006 and presented an opportunity for the country to showcase its many artistic talents

Photos: Bruce Anton

The Trinidad Theatre Workshop was established by Derek Walcott who, although born in St Lucia, lived in Trinidad from the 1950s through to the late 1970s

Photo: Stephen Broadbridge

Walcott inevitably dominates drama but Rawle Gibbons, head of the University of the West Indies' Creative Arts Centre, began a more roots-oriented indigenous genre in the 1980s with his *Sing D Chorus* trilogy, chronicling Trinidad's development from colony to independent nation with lyrics culled from classic calypso. His 1993 adaptation of C.L.R. James's *Black Jacobins* was a major statement of pan-Caribbean Creole sensibility and aesthetics. The young playwright, Davlin Thomas produces his own plays on a regular basis while London-based Mustapha Matura has registered his mark on the British theatrical establishment with original works like *Play Mas* and *Rum an' Coca Cola* as well as adaptations like *Playboy of the West Indies*.

Dance legacy

With its multi-heritage, Trinidad and Tobago has a vibrant dance tradition, embracing classical Indian, African (kalenda, bongo, limbo, ibo, pique, manding, congo, juba, hallicord) and Creole dance (bele, Grenade, biguine). The late Beryl McBurnie, founder of the Little Carib Theatre (1948), is rightfully known as the 'Mother of Caribbean Dance' for her researches into preservation and promotion of Caribbean folk forms from right across the region. Thanks to McBurnie, Trinidad's 'Best Village' competition was founded in the 1960s, keeping folk dance alive. Her legacy is maintained by contemporary choreographers like Carol la Chapelle, Heather Gordon-Henderson and Noble Douglas. Astor Johnson's modern dance company shaped many dancers who went on to achieve international fame in the 1970s and 80s.

Pieces from the masters

In the visual arts, Trinidad can boast one of the earliest masters of Caribbean art – Jean Michel Cazabon (1813-88). This son of wealthy, free coloured planters from Martinique, left an important collection of luminous watercolour landscapes. An arts scene only began developing in the early twentieth century with the 1929 foundation of the Society of Independents, a group of upper class artists including painter Hugh Stollmeyer and illustrator Amy Pang. The Independents inspired a generation of younger artists like the multi-talented Boscoe Holder, who, after a glittering career in Europe, returned to Trinidad in 1962 to become the leading society painter.

Astor Johnson's modern dance company shaped many dancers who went on to achieve international fame in the 1970s and 1980s

Photo: Andrea De Silva

Carnival designer, Peter Minshall
Photo: Shirley Bahadur

The Trinidad Art Society, founded in 1943, continued the pioneering work of the Independents in establishing a national art movement. Leading figures included Sybil Atteck, and younger artists like Carlisle Chang, Nina Lamming and Leo Glasgow.

In the first flush of Independence, the government provided the kind of support for the arts which is the envy of today's artists. Murals by Atteck and Chang were commissioned and collections set up.

During the 1960s, Isaiah James Boodoo and Sonnylal Rambissoon emerged and began exploring the Indian heritage. Pat Chu Foon, partly trained by legendary copper-worker Ken Morris, produced such iconic monumental statues as that of Gandhi in San Fernando and the Mt Hope 'Mother and Child'. The Black Power consciousness of the 1970s inspired a rediscovery of African heritage, notably in the work of Leroy Clarke whose ongoing project 'The Poet' has contributed a dense body of intricate visual imagery to the national vision.

With his Hummingbird design for the 1974 carnival, Peter Minshall burst on the local and subsequently the international scene, designing the opening ceremonies for the Barcelona Olympics and the World Cup football competition. Other artists who have made international reputations include abstract painter Ken Crichlow and assemblage sculptor Francisico Cabral. Watercolourists Noel Vaucrosson and Jackie Hinkson continue Cazabon's legacy, while the avant garde scene has been led since the 1990s by a loose group of multi-media artists including Eddie Bowen, Chris Cozier and Steve Ouditt along with new-bloods Mario Lewis and Dean Arlen. A number of women are now prominent: sculptor Anna Serrao, figurative painter Irene Shaw and Wendy Nanan.

Developing film-making

When it comes to the silver screen, Trinidad and Tobago has, to date, served as exotic location rather than a local industry centre. The 1952 film, *Affair in Trinidad*, featuring Rita Hayworth and Glen Ford, and more recently (2001), the Ismail Merchant adaptation of V.S. Naipaul's *The Mystic Masseur*, was shot entirely on location in Tucker Valley, Chaguaramas, using local and international talent.

However, in the early 1970s, Harbance Kumar laid the foundation of a fledgling industry with his movies *The Right and Wrong*, *The Caribbean Fox* (both 1970) and then *Bim* (1974), scripted by writer and journalist Raoul Pantin, with music by Andre Tanker and starring then schoolteacher, later 1990s Cabinet Minister, Ralph Maraj. The latter is now recognised as a classic of Caribbean cinema.

Trini actors who have made international names for themselves in film include Errol Sitahal, who has had roles in a number of Hollywood productions – *The Little Princess* (1995), *Harold & Kumar Go To White Castle* (2004) and Michael Cherrie who played the lead in a TV adaptation of Caryl Phillips's *The Final Passage* (1996). In the 1990s, two martial arts cum-cops-and-corruption movies, *Men of Gray*, were shot locally using a local cast and directed by US-based Anthony Joseph.

Belmont-born Trini, Horace Ové, based in London since the 1960s, is recognised as the Anglophone Caribbean's leading and most prolific film maker, he's also credited by the British Film Institute as "a pioneer in Black British history", his work providing "a perspective on the Black experience in Britain". He is cited in the *Guinness Book of Records* as the first Caribbean director of a Black feature film (*Pressure*, 1973), which was co-scripted with fellow Trini, Sam Selvon, and he is also known as the first Caribbean director of an independently produced documentary (*Reggae*, 1973).

The future of Trinidad and Tobago film seems to rest in the hands of the innovative film-maker, Yao Ramesar who has been winning international awards for his documentaries on Trinidad and Tobago culture since the 1990s and whose first feature, *SistaGod*, premiered at the 2006 Toronto Film Festival. ■

The two faces of the capital

KRIS RAMPERSAD

Almost one century to the day since Port of Spain saw its first architectural blossoming, the city's façade is metamorphosing into a character befitting this new millennium.

Its changing façade is comparable only to the architectural flowering at the turn of the 20th century. This saw the altering of the landscape in the first decade of the 20th century – largely between 1902 and 1909 – to accommodate the 'Magnificent Seven' along the Queen's Park Savannah, with Knowsley, and Boissiere House (the gingerbread house) on Queen's Park West.

The 'Magnificent Seven' – Stollmeyer's 'Castle' (Killarney), White Hall, Archbishop's House, Hayes Court, Queen's Royal College, Mille Fleurs (Prada House) and Ambard's House (Roomor) – which continue to gaze on the Savannah and occasionally glance sideways at the Northern Range, are a counterpoint to the other end of the city, which is rising to the challenges of the new age.

Sitting at the edge of the Gulf of the Paria, is the city centre. Here, the cool wooden and stone structures of the last century – some destroyed by fire, some torn down following natural deterioration – are giving way to glass and steel-fronted edifices that tower to the skies. They are complemented by a new face to what may now be called Bankers' Row between Frederick and Abercromby Streets on both north and south sides of the Brian Lara Promenade.

New structures, including an expanded port and the headquarters for the Association of Caribbean States (ACS), promise to further alter a skyscape which has already changed with the recent addition of the Nicholas Tower.

Sitting among them and around the city are some of the structures reminiscent of times past – the Catholic gothic-styled Cathedral of the Immaculate Conception, built in 1832; the Anglican Cathedral Church of the Holy Trinity, built in 1818; the Red House, built in 1907, with its ceiling of Wedgwood blue and white gesso work; and the now hollowed out frame of the old police headquarters built in 1876.

The structures of the last century, particularly those around the Savannah, are in keeping with those times, when the representation of prosperity was through lavish-styled homes that reflected the leisured-lifestyle of their owners. The 21st century reflects largely commercial expansion. These new buildings in the city pronounce on this fast-paced age of enterprise, industry and global-spiritedness.

Where the age of the last century lived with its environment, conversing through its architectural grandeur with the land on which it sits, the city's new buildings mirror the skies to dialogue with the outer universe. The builders of the Savannah masterpieces drew materials from the natural environment, while today's structures are a celebration of metal and glass.

The stretch of the city contained between Riverside Plaza and the Twin Tower is now extended further westwards with Movie Towne, the Marriot, BHP Billiton headquarters, the Jean Pierre Complex and the National Stadium creating a border with the Diego Martin hills. The expansion has virtually absorbed Woodbrook. Once a sprawling city suburb, this district is now only a scattering of family homes amid many

ABOVE: President's House
Photo: Stephen Broadbridge

FACING PAGE
Located on Independence Square,
Nicholas Tower is the tallest building in
the English-speaking Caribbean
Photo: Shirley Bahadur

business premises, restaurants and fast food outlets. The suburbs are now behind the Movie Towne to National Stadium border to West Moorings.

With such focus on the skyline, it may be easy to forget that virtually all of what is now considered the city centre once belonged to the sea. The Gulf of Paria washed along the feet of the Cathedral, and came up as far as the south side of the Promenade, before successive spates of reclamation. Altering the city's layout began with the 1787 diversion of the Dry River eastward to facilitate the kind of expansion being seen westwards.

The first phase of reclamation began in 1803 with sea lots that were only laid bare at low tide. The lots were laid out between Independence Square North (then known as King Street) and the sea, with owners developing their own plots and paying towards road-building all the way to St Vincent Street. By this means, Independence Square (then Marine Square) was developed. The second phase, in the 1840s, involved the wharf extension from the St Vincent Jetty and extension of Chacon, Frederick, Henry and Charlotte Streets across Marine Square to South Quay.

The third phase of reclamation, in 1906, took over the sea which covered the entire corner between St Vincent Street to the Furness Withy Building.

Then, no environmentally-conscious citizens lay in the way of reclamation of the Laventille Swamp on which the Beetham Highway was built in 1920. The Deepwater Harbour Scheme of 1935 brought into being the waterfront along Wrightson Road.

ABOVE: Trinity Anglican Cathedral in
Port of Spain was built in 1818
Photo: Shirley Bahadur

This area was, until then, washed by the sea. It became known as Docksite and during the Second World War, was occupied by American soldiers.

Where Independence Square intersects with the soon-to-be built Wrightson Road area was Stinking Corner. Occupied by the Furness Withy Building, next to the Unit Trust Building and the soon-to-be headquarters of the ACS, with associated walk-over to the expanding port, no one looking at that corner now – with its Times Square-like flashing billboards – could envision it being called 'Stinking Corner' and an area of mud and slush.

But such is what a century of human occupation can do to a place. Port of Spain now wears two faces. The face of the last century contemplates the still lush greenery of the Northern Range, and the reconstructed face of this century, stares out to sea, inviting in the age of globalisation. ■

ABOVE: The entrance to St James
Photo: Ian Brierley

RIGHT: 'Knowsley' is home to the
Ministry of Foreign Affairs
Photo: Stephen Broadbridge

FACING PAGE
Fort George overlooking Port of Spain
Photo: Bruce Anton

Queen's Royal
College
Photo: Bruce Anton

ABOVE: MovieTowne is the leading entertainment and shopping complex in the Caribbean. Along with its ten-screen, state of the art Cineplex, it includes a shopping mall, restaurants, bars and arcades

RIGHT: ????
Photo: Shirley Bahadur

FACING PAGE
Along with Nicholas Tower, the 'Twin Towers' dominate the capital's skyline
Photo: Stephen Broadbridge

Port of Spain
Harbour
Photo: Shirley Bahadur

ABOVE: Whitehall is the current office of
the Prime Minister
Photo: Stephen Broadbridge

RIGHT: Jinnah Mosque in St Joseph
Photo: Shirley Bahadur

FACING PAGE
The Falls at Westmall is located just
outside Port of Spain. With more than
130 world-class retail outlets and a food
court, it is one of the Caribbean's leading
shopping malls
Photo: Stephen Broadbridge

PREVIOUS PAGES
The Cenotaph in Memorial Park
Photo: Bruce Anton

Cathedral of the Immaculate Conception
in Independence Square
Photo: Shirley Bahadur

RIGHT: The 'Twin Towers' and Nicholas Tower are an imposing sight above Port of Spain
Photo: Shirley Bahadur

City Hall and bandstand in San Fernando
Photo: Stephen Broadbridge

The changing tempo of San Fernando

KRIS RAMPERSAD

One may say without fear of contradiction that south Trinidad in general, and San Fernando in particular, is the incubator for leaders of Trinidad and Tobago in all spheres of life. Two of the country's four prime ministers and two of its four presidents were born in the south. Current President, George Maxwell Richards, former President Noor Hassanali, current Prime Minister Patrick Manning and former Prime Minister Basdeo Panday, have roots in south Trinidad and strong ties to San Fernando. Among the city's other noteworthy sons are Olympic Gold Medal winner, Hasely Crawford, long-distance runner Manny Ramjohn, golfer Stephen Ames and steelbandsman extraordinaire, Liam Teague.

Known as the country's southern capital, and endowed with city status in 1988, San Fernando is located in Naparima. This name was derived from its original Carib name, Anaparima, meaning 'without water', despite the fact that the Cipero, Marabella, Godineau and Vistabella Rivers pass through the district. Two other major rivers flow past its north and south – Guaracara and Oropouche – respectively, and it is washed by the Gulf of Paria to the west. However, it may be that the country's first inhabitants were considering the undulating land which, like a duck's back, does not hold water. Some of the rivers drain into the Navet Dam, one of the main reservoirs that supply potable water to the city and outlying southern districts, which also doubles as a delightful picnic area. Some of this can be viewed from the park atop the hill that surveys the lowlands beneath.

The Southern Main Road, which begins in Curepe, ends in San Fernando. To the city's east, running north-south is the Sir Solomon Hochoy Highway, named after the last governor of Trinidad. It connects through the historic White Bridge in Cipero to the South Trunk Road that meanders into the heavy industrial areas of oil and gas extraction.

Hence, San Fernando is also known as the industrial capital of Trinidad, vis-à-vis the administrative capital of Port of Spain. Asserting this status, at its south-western end, is the now relatively idle Usine Ste Madeleine Sugar Factory – blackened by decades of sugar production. Amid the rolling hills of the Sugar Belt, it is a symbol of the changing fortunes of not just the city, but the country; testimony to the era when sugar was king and when extensive plantations dominated the southern landscape, on which the town grew, drawing sustenance from the fertile soils of the Naparima plains.

New fortunes have been founded in the petroleum, natural gas and energy related industries that now fuel not only world economies, but also world politics. San Fernando's commanding landmark now is the Petrotrin Oil Refinery – towering elegant steel towers glinting in the tropical sun and straddling the city's entrance, eastwards towards Marabella and Gulf of Paria. Thus, it claims its place as the main driver of the city's development in the last half a century, and the wealth-producing part of the island.

High Street, an offshoot of the convergence of the Southern Main Road, and the Naparima Road at Library Corner with its architecturally refined Carnegie Free Library, runs through the city centre. This, the city's main thoroughfare, escapes the bustle of

Trinidad's second capital seen from San Fernando Hill
Photo: Shirley Bahadur

ABOVE: White Bridge in Cipero

FACING PAGE: San Fernando Hill

Photos: Shirley Bahadur

human and vehicular traffic in a winding downward sweep to the quiet calm of the Gulf, almost envious of the parallel St James Street that skirts the bustle towards the Gulf. The city breathes through the Harris Promenade, a neatly manicured park with its monumental engine of the last train to San Fernando sitting in its foreground which ends before the colonial-styled, and imposing San Fernando General Hospital.

San Fernando's best-kept secret must be that it remains one of the most breathtaking parts of the island. Accessed through the Highway, its modulating hills and valleys that stretch to the sea escape the average visitor or commuter. But a drive through the lesser-trodden paths of the city can yield enormous visual surprises – a feast to the eyes of the sparkling Gulf hidden just behind the last hill, or new high-rise residential block.

The Naparima Bowl, the city's performing arts centre is complemented by entertainment, concerts, trade shows and Carnival competitions. Major sporting tournaments, held at Skinners' Park, have now been decentralised to the new Manny Ramjohn Stadium on the north-eastern corner, and Guaracara Park to the south west.

San Fernando enjoys a vibrant Carnival season, rivalled only by the capital city's among world Carnivals. Fetes at Skinners' Park, Guaracara Park, the Petrotrin Sports Club, the San Fernando Yacht Club, among others, precede the two days of fun and frolic to the tempo of steelband and calypso, soca and chutney music. In fact, Skinners' Park has been the Waterloo of many a calypso, soca, or chutney artiste as their audiences passionately demonstrate endorsement (by applause), or rejection (by waving streams of toilet paper). It can make or break an artiste, so much so that it has developed the reputation, "if Skinner Park say so, is so". ■

The Petrotrin Oil
Refinery is San
Fernando's most
commanding
landmark
Photo: Shirley Bahadur

All roads lead to Chaguanas

KRIS RAMPERSAD

The phenomenal growth rate of Chaguanas in the last few decades – from village to town to borough – makes it one of the most desirable places to live and do business in Trinidad. Nearly 100,000 of Trinidad's 1.3 million people make this district their home.

Located within the sprawling plains of what was known, until recently, as the green sugar belt along the Sir Solomon Hochoy Highway and the Southern Main Road, is a vortex to Port of Spain, San Fernando, Piarco International Airport and Point Lisas. It embraces such districts as Charlieville, Chase Village, Felicity, Lange Park, Montrose, Edinburgh, Endeavour, Carlsen Field, Enterprise and Cunupia.

The district is traversed by the Caroni River, which allowed British explorers to sail upriver to capture the country's first capital, San Jose De Aruna (St Joseph), from the Spanish. The river has since become a symbol of the North-South divide that cities tend to adopt that feed the friendly contest between rural and urban competition for resources and recognition.

The river leads into the Caroni Swamp, an area protected by the International Ramesar Convention on Wetlands of World Significance. Here nests the scarlet ibis, the national bird of Trinidad and Tobago. The spectacle of seeing hundreds of these red birds flying in to roost against the late afternoon sky has been a popular attraction for nationals and visitors alike.

A large part of the general attractiveness of Chaguanas for residence and commercial activity has little to do with the proximity of the scarlet ibis, and more with its easy accessibility to and from all areas of the country. Within the main area, the Chaguanas Main Road links the nearby districts from the swamp through Charlieville, Felicity to Longdenville, Claxton Bay and Freeport. The north-south Southern Main Road provides a direct route to Piarco International Airport to its east and the Point Lisas Industrial Estate and San Fernando to the west. This is complemented by the Sir Solomon Hochoy Highway, which intersects the east-west Churchill Roosevelt Highway, taking travellers from Chaguaramas to Toco.

A comprehensive range of transport modes, from private vehicles to public buses, maxi taxis and taxis facilitate movement for residents, most of whom work in the capital.

New commercial interests have been targeting the outskirts of the traditional borough centre in anticipation of continued growth with such housing development schemes as Orchard Gardens, Lange Park and Edinburgh Gardens. This outward expansion has added the sprawling Price Plaza and the Food Basket at its northern entrance to the several malls that already serve shoppers – Mid-Centre Mall, Center City and Centre Pointe Malls.

Such interest in the borough has resulted in rapid increases in the value and price of real estate though it remains comparatively more affordable than the congested capital city and its suburbs. With the planned release of lands previously reserved for sugar cane and agricultural production, even greater development of the built environment is expected.

Mid Centre Mall, top left; Chaguanas
Main Road, above; Chaguanas Market,
main picture

Photos: Shirley Bahadur

Lion House, right, is one of Trinidad's
most famous landmarks

Photo: Kris Rampersad

The focus on outward development has largely allowed the borough centre to retain its character as a veritable bazaar that includes a combination of pavement shopping and in-store air conditioned facilities in some of the island's major chain stores as well as privately-run small businesses. This centre runs largely east to west, spilling into some north-south streets from Montrose to the Chaguanas market, close to which is located the police station and the courthouse.

On the western edge of this shopping district is located one of Trinidad's most famous landmarks – the Lion House – made famous by the borough's most renowned son, Nobel Laureate, Sir Vidia Naipaul. Immortalised in his epic West Indian novel, *A House for Mr Biswas* (as Hanuman House), the house was built by the Capildeo family. Literary and other enthusiasts can visit the house, and even request a tour of the structure that has been described in intimate detail in the novel.

Other sons with international prominence in their fields are cricketer, Dinanath Ramnarine and footballer, Scott Sealy who, incidentally, were born on the same day, six years apart.

Born on 4 June 1975, Ramnarine represented Trinidad and Tobago and the West Indies at Test match level. He retired in 2002 at the age of 28. Born on the same day in 1981, Sealy now plays in Major League Soccer for the Kansas City Wizards in the United States. He played with the Trinidad and Tobago national team in the 2006 World Cup qualifying match against Mexico. ∎

In the footsteps of 'big sister'

KRIS RAMPERSAD

In an era past of more rigid gender definitions and a less strident anti-smoking lobby, tobacco, the pipe through which it is smoked, and the smell of it being smoked, all implied the intensely masculine. Yet it is evident that Tobago, Trinidad's 'sister', conjures up only the feminine.

The logo of the Tobago Heritage Festival is of a pregnant woman in silhouette, with the declaration, "She becomes more beautiful". Save for the jealousy of one female (Hurricane Flora), hurricanes from the Atlantic kiss, but rarely ravish her, rather, venting their wrath on those higher up the Leeward Islands. Robinson Crusoe sought shelter in her bosom, and some even claim that she conceals a secret passage to the Lost City of Atlantis.

Named by the indigenous Taino tribe ('Tabago', the tribal name for the tobacco pipe), she is the Cleopatra of Caribbean islands. Petite at just 300 sq km (116 sq miles), she has seduced conquistadors, pirates and has been one of the most fought-over of colonial territories. So desirable has she been that she changed hands many times from one European coloniser to the next – 'founded' by Spain; occupied by the Dutch; coveted by Sweden and Poland; annexed by Courlandians (Courland was a dukedom within what is now the Republic of Latvia); settled by the French; and ruled by Britain until she was warded to Trinidad in 1899.

Though Columbus never touched her, it is believed at first sight he named her Belaforma, and she remained the mistress of the Tainos who fiercely protected her against a British attempt at settlement in the early 17th century. The Dutch, who called her New Wascheral, were more successful, setting up a settlement in the first quarter of the century and within the next twenty years, Courlandians followed suit. Both the Dutch and Courlandians claimed her, until the Dutch overpowered the Courlandians in the mid-17th century. Poland and Sweden unsuccessfully fought for her. Some ten years later she was a prize the Dutch gave to France, but repossessed within another decade. Having had a taste of possession, the French duelled with the Dutch and took her a couple years later. It was not long before Courland again claimed ownership, but the French defended successfully. The exhausted and embattled Europeans needed a reprieve and declared her neutral territory in the mid-eighteenth century. France made her a peace offering to Britain in 1763, but seized her again in 1781 until Britain successfully fought back in 1793. The 1802 Treaty of Amiens passed her to France who, during the Napoleonic Wars, ceded her to Britain, and in 1899 Britain annexed her to Trinidad.

In recent times, Tobago has given the Republic of Trinidad and Tobago a Prime Minister and President in the shape of A.N.R. Robinson.

The many forts dotting the island stand guard over its history with Europe. Fort King George in the capital, Scarborough, guards the town with its command of the spectacular coast that unfolds in the brightest blue that makes it indistinguishable from the sky above. Its narrow streets wind precariously down to the town centre, where houses and shops are perched precipitously on the edges of the roads as if reaching out to draw customers to their goods. Not too far below, the harbour is in constant flux with the to and fro of goods and passengers.

Perched on a hilltop, the Tobago House of Assembly, the semi-autonomous body charged with administering the needs of the island, oversees not only the capital, but all of Tobago.

Between July and August, all can take part in the Tobago Heritage Festival. The island-wide event is an exposition of drumming, music, storytelling, song, poetry, dance and drama, which taps into the uniqueness of each of the villages.

One can become a child again, sitting at the feet of the storytelling grandmother – from Les Coteau village which is buried deep in a valley of surrounding dark green vegetation. She who converses not only with the dead pirates and adventurers of old, but also the spirits that inhabit the land: dowens, soucouyants, la diablesse, papa bois and mama l'eau. Those who prefer more everyday fantasies, may participate in the Tobago Wedding hosted by Mount Moriah. The event comes complete with the village gossipmonger who vents the closet scandals on the bride, groom and their families. In fact, many visitors choose to make Tobago the setting for their own weddings. Then join in the dances where African meets European heritage in the Tobago Jig; or dance the reel, bele, pique, quadrille, polka and waltz to the music of the tambrin drums and fiddle.

Amid the Heritage Festival is the now well-established Tobago Jazz Festival, which draws in both home-grown and international singers and musicians.

In September, Tobago Fest celebrates its familial ties with Trinidad and the Trinidad

TOP: Heritage Festival dancers
Photo: Tobago Tourism Authority

ABOVE: Dapper guest at a traditional
Moriah wedding ceremony
Photo: Clement Williams

MAIN PICTURE
Red and blue devils at the Tobago
Carnival
Photo: Clement Williams

ABOVE: Goat racing at Buccoo
Photo: Clement Williams

BELOW: Fine cuisine is a speciality at Le Grand Courlan Spa Resort located at Stonehaven Bay

Carnival with its own J'Ouvert, Parade of the Bands, crowning of a Fest Queen and soca and steelband competitions.

Tobago's natural history holds its own treasury of surprises. Its 210 species of bird, 17 species of mammal, 23 species of butterfly and many species of reptile, find a protective haven in the expansive Tobago Forest Reserve. This rainforest area spans the breath of the island around its middle and is also home to spectacular waterfalls and hiking trails.

Just off Tobago's coast is Little Tobago, also known as Bird of Paradise Island. In 1909, Sir William Ingram introduced the species to the island from New Guinea. However, it is believed that the entire population was wiped out by Hurricane Flora in 1963. Today, the island's total area of one square kilometre provides adequate food and shelter for several of Tobago's wildlife species.

The waters around Little Tobago and nearby Goat Island provide a haven for a spectacular array of marine life. It is a Mecca for the world's scuba divers and is home to the largest brain coral in the world: Kelleston Drain.

On any given day, one can take an early morning walk along the beach, help fishermen pull in their nets, or even glimpse a whale spouting water way out to sea. And at the close of day, settle down for the vista of one of Tobago's stunning sunsets from the shores of Store Bay.

Of all the events taking place on the island, none stirs the imagination more than the goat and crab races. Held during the long Easter weekend, these popular events are open to adults and children who feel their creature stands a chance of crossing the finish line in first place. Goat races have been held on 'Easter Tuesday' since 1925 and are an adjunct to Easter Monday horse racing.

Tobago may be the reserved, laid back sister, but some of Trinidad's vivacity has certainly rubbed off. ∎

ABOVE:
Overlooking Store
Bay, and set within
seven acres of
landscaped
grounds, Crown
Point Beach Hotel
offers studio
accommodation
and apartments, all
with spectacular
views of the
Caribbean Sea

RIGHT: Pirates Bay
at Charlotteville
Photo: Andrea De Silva

Support for the nation's football team, throughout its journey to the
2006 World Cup finals in Germany, was in true carnival fashion

Photo: Ian Brierley

Inspirational sporting achievements

FAZEER MOHAMMED

Long before achieving independence from the United Kingdom in 1962, the people of Trinidad and Tobago had taken pride in the sporting exploits of sons and daughters of the soil, especially in the global competitive arenas. Such successes and achievements are regarded as reflective of their worth as a nation and a people capable of making some form of impact on the international scene.

With a sporting culture influenced heavily by the legacy of British colonialism, it was inevitable that cricket, football and athletics would be at the very foundation of the Trinidad and Tobago sporting experience, producing the bulk of the country's outstanding individual performers and team achievements. These range from the swashbuckling exploits of flamboyant all-rounder, Learie Constantine in the fledgling years of West Indies Test cricket in the 1920s, to the historic appearance of the national football team – the Soca Warriors – at the 2006 World Cup finals in Germany.

Yet, while public interest and participation in these sports are understandably greater, the scope of sporting involvement in the country is as wide as it is deep, encompassing almost every established discipline, except those related to temperate climates, for obvious reasons.

Say, "Trinidad and Tobago" in any sporting debate anywhere in the world, and names like Brian Lara, Dwight Yorke and Ato Boldon will crop up among contemporary achievers on the international stage.

Brian Lara is the country's first, true cricketing superstar. He has established new standards in batsmanship in an international career that began in 1990 and which is expected to come to an end some time after the 2007 Cricket World Cup in the Caribbean. This left-hander has exhibited phenomenal run-scoring, encompassing records for the highest individual scores in Test and first-class cricket and the most career runs by a batsman in Test history. The distinctive style and flair with which his records have been achieved have earned him a unique iconic status in his homeland. If he manages to lead the West Indies to success in his farewell World Cup appearance on regional soil, then his status will surely be elevated to an almost celestial level.

Like Lara, Dwight Yorke is coming to the end of a distinguished sporting career, with the World Cup experience in Germany being the high-point for him and fellow veterans, Russell Latapy, Shaka Hislop and Stern John. As a son of Tobago, Yorke, wearing the captain's armband, made it an even greater honour by warming the hearts of those of the sister isle who sustain a lingering resentment towards Trinidad for what they perceive to be marginalisation and occasional disregard for their issues in the national scheme of things. Yorke had already done it all at club level with England's Manchester United – arguably the most popular team in world sport – and his value as a player, even nearing the end of his career, is evidenced by his success in Australia in leading Sydney to the inaugural A-League Championship in 2005.

Hasely Crawford remains the nation's lone achiever of an Olympic gold medal for his triumph in the men's 100 metres at the 1976 Games in Montreal. However, Ato

Soca Warriors
(L-R): Captain,
Dwight Yorke,
formerly of
Manchester
United; Russell
Latapy, who
plays for Falkirk
in Scotland; and
Stern John, who
represents
English club,
Coventry City
Photos: Ian Brierley

Boldon's achievements in more than a decade of competition at the highest level for Trinidad and Tobago have made him the country's most successful ambassador in the sport. The sprinter's tally of one silver and three bronze medals at successive Olympics (1996 and 2000) is, in itself, worthy of lofty commendation. Yet his status as the country's most consistent performer is fully revealed by a glance at his other successes. These include a World Championship triumph over 200 metres, gold over 100 metres at the Commonwealth Games, double success at the World Junior level, and a succession of impressive performances on the Grand Prix circuit where he made a habit of running under ten seconds for the 100 metres, and under 20 seconds for the 200 metres at the same track meeting.

But long before Crawford and Boldon came on the scene, Trinidad and Tobago's flag was being hoisted at Olympic level through the efforts of Rodney Wilkes and Lennox Kilgour in weightlifting in the 1950s. More recently, the country's lone medallist at the 2004 Games in Athens, George Bovell III (bronze in the men's 200-metre individual medley), is the first ever Olympic medallist in the swimming pool for the English-speaking Caribbean.

This variety of world-class sporting talent extends to boxing, where a golden period in the 1980s brought two world champions in the shape of Claude Noel in the lightweight division and Leslie Stewart in the light-heavyweight category. And in netball, the country aspires to a return to the glory years that culminated with a share of the world title alongside New Zealand and Australia when the tournament was hosted by Trinidad and Tobago in 1979.

Even if the degree of public interest and participation is nowhere near the level of the more popular sports, this nation of just 1.3 million people has produced performers who have conquered the world in their specific disciplines. Through his exploits in Europe and the United States, highlighted by victory at the Tournament Players' Championship in 2006, Stephen Ames (who is now a Canadian citizen) has established a niche for the land of his birth in the world of golf – more than twenty years after teenager, Maria Nunes claimed a junior world title. Like Nunes, Darrem Charles was a world junior champion in the field of bodybuilding, and continues to feature on the United States professional circuit.

Essentially, the story of Trinidad and Tobago on the regional and international sporting stage is similar to that of many young nations, where the combination of tradition and greater opportunities in certain disciplines have produced constant successes, while less popular events have seen more sporadic achievements.

However, the underlying theme of it all is that the country has always been blessed with abundant natural talent; from barefooted distance runner, Mannie Ramjohn and world record-holding sprinter, MacDonald Bailey in the days before independence, to

George Bovell III is the first ever Olympic medallist in the swimming pool for the English-speaking Caribbean
Photo: Shirley Bahadur

Hasley Crawford Stadium, above
Photo: Shirley Bahadur

Photo: Andrea De Silva

Race day at Arima
Photo: Shirley Bahadur

the likes of new World Junior athletics champions, Renny Quow (400 metres) and Rhonda Watkins (high jump). If cricket and football are, by some distance, the most prominent of team sports, they take nothing away from the regional successes over the years in basketball, volleyball and hockey.

In the face of the widening scourge of drug abuse and a rising tide of crime and violence, Trinidad and Tobago, like many other Caribbean nations, is recognising the value of sport. Not only is it a source of national pride and a revenue-earning medium but also, more importantly, it is a means for channelling youthful energy towards positive, disciplined pursuits that can contribute to the benefit of the country in more ways than one.

Of course, with the Cricket World Cup coming to the Caribbean in 2007, Trinidad and Tobago is also mobilising to make the most of the event both financially and

infrastructurally. Interestingly, the government had chosen not to engage in the costly redevelopment required to host matches in the latter stages of the tournament, believing that the considerable costs would not have brought long-term returns to justify such expenditure as the country is not nearly as well established as other Caribbean territories in the tourism market.

Nevertheless, the hosting of preliminary group matches involving India, Sri Lanka, Bangladesh and Bermuda is sure to attract enough international spectator interest and, therefore, myriad financial opportunities at all levels to produce a surge of economic activity in the weeks and months leading up to those matches in March 2007.

In more ways than one, sport is a big thing in Trinidad and Tobago, and the country will no doubt continue to look to this aspect of social life for inspiration, international validation and enrichment, both on and off the field of play. ■

Terrific for tourism

ELSPETH DUNCAN / PHOTOS BY STEPHEN BROADBRIDGE

The stereotypical notion of 'twins', given their shared genetic component, is that they are exactly alike. The twin islands of Trinidad and Tobago, located seven miles off the coast of Venezuela, share the genetic component of the South American continent, of which they were once a part. As a result, their main similarities are ecological, both possessing the unique diversity of both South American and Antillean ecosystems – unlike other Caribbean islands. From rainforests to mountains to swamplands, the islands, with their high species to area ratio, are collectively bursting with an easily accessible and diverse range of continental flora and fauna.

However, 21 miles apart from each other, the twin islands also have their differences. Trinidad, the larger of the two (at 1,864 sq miles compared with Tobago's 116 sq miles), is quick to party, don sequins and feathers for Carnival, seal the next industrial or commercial business deal and lead a faster-paced life. Tobago, not as interested in keeping apace with the intense cultural, industrial and economic energy of her sister isle, remains relaxed and laid back, happy to spend days hiking, snorkelling and scuba diving, or lounging on a beach soaking in lazy sunsets.

Positioned largely as a prime destination for leisure, event and conference tourism, these two islands present a vast range of assorted tourism treats to both foreigners and nationals – the latter being increasingly courted through maximised efforts to promote 'home' as a worthy holiday destination and increase the awareness of tourism as a viable industry.

Annual visitor arrivals to Trinidad and Tobago for the first five years of this millennium ranged from 398,559 in 2005 to 460,195 in 2005, with rough percentages indicating the preferred reasons for visiting: 35 percent leisure and beach, 27 percent visiting friends and relatives, eighteen percent business, fifteen percent other, three percent weddings and honeymoons, and one percent study.

Government policy and administration

The job of marketing Trinidad and Tobago and elevating the tourism sector to internationally competitive standards lies largely in the hands of the state-owned Tourism Development Company (TDC). The road being paved towards tourism '2020' (the government's projected date for the achievement of 'developed country status') follows strategic directions, among them: the implementation of new rooms and upgrading of existing room stock to international standards; the upgrading of various tourist sites and attractions; increased air service to both islands; enhancement of industry quality and standards through training of service personnel; and the raising of the level of tourism awareness among citizens.

For any island that aims for 'developed country status' and internationally competitive tourism standards, one of the first steps to success comes through its people caring for and valuing its indigenous treasures. This takes on a deeper meaning when one considers that a vast segment of Trinidad and Tobago's indigenous tourism treasure trove exists within the environment.

ABOVE: Boat trip through
the Caroni Swamp

Award-winning wildlife
photographer, Stephen
Broadbridge, through his
company Caribbean
Discovery Tours, brings
Trinidad's virtually untouched
forest and swamp up-close
and personal. The
conservationist's enthusiasm
and knowledge of the subject
makes for an unforgettable
wildlife experience. Clients of
Caribbean Discovery Tours
include family groups,
adventure-travellers,
universities, filmmakers and
both local and international
television crews.

Eco-Tourism

Eco-tourism is one of the fastest growing forms of tourism in the Caribbean. However, while nature-based tourism can be 'eco-sensitive' and intent on creating a comfortable and memorable experience for the average nature-lover, true eco-tourism is a more conscious form of nature tourism. It is responsible, sustainable tourism that minimizes impact on the environment as much as possible, involves local communities (sustainable social development) and reinvests its profits into environmental conservation. This educated and respectful approach to nature is necessary in order to preserve the very product that draws people to these twin islands.

National Parks

Once a visitor to these islands has even the remotest interest in natural history, a guaranteed good place to start looking for 'eco-action' is in any of the national parks. These designated areas play a vital role in the protection of zones which contain significant examples of the country's flora and fauna.

Matura National Park, a 9,000-hectare natural wonderland, contains a large area populated by mora trees, some of which tower as high as forty metres. These evergreen forests, estimated to be 30,000 years old, contain a world of ecological treasures. The rare and endangered orchid, *oncidium citrinum*, and the endemic pawi are two examples of the exotic to be found in this protected area.

AT A GLANCE

VISITORS

Leisure & beach	35%
Visiting friends & relatives	27%
Business	18%
Weddings & honeymoons	3%
Study	1%
Other	15%

El Tucuche Mountain which, at around 3000ft, is Trinidad's second highest peak

THE NATURAL WORLD UP CLOSE

Trinidad and Tobago Sightseeing Tours is the country's leading tour company and provides services on both islands from Destination Management, Incentive and Conference services, Eco Adventure, Sports and a host of other tourism related services, as well providing shore excursions for a large number of Cruise Lines and hotel reservations. Its destination management company ensures an exhilarating and knowledge-based touring experience through trained guides and support personnel. In an industry where attention to detail is of utmost importance, Trinidad & Tobago Sightseeing Tours considers the tour guide one of the finest points in creating an excellent experience for guests.

ABOVE: Yellow, or golden, poui tree in bloom

FACING PAGE
Southern Range mountains in Trinidad

The ocelot, red howler monkey, yellow-crowned parrot, bearded bell bird, bullfinch and picoplat (all threatened species), make their homes alongside wild game species such as red brocket deer, lappe, tattoo, matte, tayra, iguana and wild hog. In light of the range of interesting flora and fauna and the threat of over-hunting, Matura was proclaimed an Environmentally Sensitive Area (ESA) and National Park.

Wetlands

In 1993, Trinidad and Tobago became a signatory to the Ramsar Convention on Wetlands, which focuses nationally and internationally on the conservation and wise use of wetlands and their resources. The three sites designated as Wetlands of International Importance are Buccoo Reef / Bon Accord Lagoon Complex in Tobago and the Caroni and Nariva Swamps in Trinidad.

The Caroni Swamp, another popular national park and vast wetland of some 8,398 hectares, is home to an impressive range of wildlife. Some twenty endangered bird species have been recorded here including the scarlet ibis, comb duck, white-tailed kite and peregrine falcon, and approximately 24 species of fish and other creatures such as crabs, caiman, oysters, snakes and silky anteaters. This swampy kingdom, dominated by red mangrove, is made up of freshwater herbaceous marshes, brackish and saline lagoons, natural and artificial channels and mudflats. A boat trip through the mangrove on an evening with Nanan's Bird Sanctuary Tours reveals the magic of a large flying red carpet in the sky, as flocks of scarlet ibis, for which the swamp is home, head to the mangrove to roost.

AT A GLANCE

FLORA
2,500 species in about 175 families

MAMMALS
100 species (including marine mammals), 9 orders and around 27 families

BIRDS
433 species, 66 families in 20 orders

REPTILES
93 species (including marine turtles)

MARINE FISH
500 species

FRESHWATER FISH
44 species

AMPHIBIANS
40 species (all frogs and toads)

BUTTERFLIES
617 species

TOP: Orange-winged Amazon parrot

MIDDLE: Fer de lance snake

BOTTOM: White tail page moth

AT A GLANCE

PROTECTED AREAS

Trinidad

Matura National Park   9,000 ha
Caroni Swamp   8,398 ha
Nariva Swamp   7,000 ha

Tobago

Buccoo Reef
Bon Accord Lagoon Complex

CLOCKWISE FROM TOP
Channel-billed toucan; opossum;
spectacled caiman; king cracker moth;
roadrunner lizard

FACING PAGE
Bamboo walkway in Chaguaramas

Remarkable eco-adventures can be experienced in Trinidad's largest freshwater herbaceous swamp, the Nariva Swamp, which occupies some 7,000 hectares. This area possesses a unique ecosystem and is one of the most important protected zones in Trinidad and Tobago. The area's freshwater marshes and swamplands, mangrove, palm swamp communities and evergreen seasonal forests provide habitats for a vast array of fauna, some of which are rare, vulnerable or endangered such as the rare Suriname toad, the vulnerable red howler monkey, the endangered manatee and blue and gold macaw. Nature enthusiasts can revel in the knowledge that this extraordinary ecosystem contains eleven species of snake, 57 species of mammal and 34 families representing 171 recorded species of bird. Nestled in the Nariva Swamp area is the virtually untouched island of 'Bush Bush' (1,600 hectares), which was made a wildlife sanctuary in 1968 and declared a prohibited area in 1989 in light of illegal activities such as poaching, hunting and fishing.

ABOVE: Immortelle tree in bloom

RIGHT: Blue crabs

TOP: White-fronted capuchin

RIGHT: Rufous-tailed jacamar

FAR RIGHT: Chestnut woodpecker

FACING PAGE
Kayaking in the Nariva Swamp

Endangered species

Certain wildlife species in Trinidad and Tobago are classified under specific categories based on the extent to which they are considered to be threatened by extinction. Endangered species, such as the ocelot, water opossum, scarlet ibis, three-toed anteater and leatherback turtle have experienced a drastic reduction in their numbers. Vulnerable species, such as the red howler monkey, white-fronted capuchin monkey, prehensile-tailed porcupine and oilbird, are under threat of becoming endangered if adequate systems are not put in place for their protection. Rare species, such as the golden tree frog, striped owl, Muscovy duck and red-capped cardinal, are those whose already small populations are considered to be at risk.

One of Trinidad's best-known wildlife sanctuaries – a bird-watcher's haven and home of the oilbird – is the internationally-acclaimed Asa Wright Nature Centre (established in 1967). The centre, located in the Northern Range of Trinidad, has at the core of its operations a commitment to reinvesting funds into the environment. Every cent made, largely through the operation of their 24-room lodge, goes directly back into its upkeep and activities: mainly conservation, community development, education, research and land acquisition for the purpose of preservation. Their clients, most of them serious conservationists, can rest assured that the money they spend goes back into the environment and surrounding communities.

CLOCKWISE FROM TOP: Great
kiskadee; pink nymphea; prehensile-
tailed porcupine; one of over six
hundred varieties of butterfly

FACING PAGE
Madamas waterfall

Diversity

Tobago, with its cool rainforests, placid lagoons and tucked away waterfalls, also enjoys a diverse array of plant, insect, reptile, bird and marine life.

Little Tobago Island, just off Speyside, is one of the prime seabird sanctuaries in the Caribbean. Clearly charmed by the ecology of the island, the English naturalist and broadcaster, David Attenborough used it as a location for his BBC documentary, *Trials of Life*. The red-footed booby, red-billed tropic bird, tropical kingbird, frigate bird and the sooty tern are among the birds that share the island as a nesting ground. Another of Tobago's protected areas, the Main Ridge rainforest, became the first example of a protected area in the Western Hemisphere when it was designated accordingly in 1764.

Off the coast of Tobago, divers can explore deep worlds of manta rays, hawksbill turtles, barracuda, sharks, sea horses, moray eels, octopuses and many other fascinating forms of marine life. However, while the island has its protected areas, various threats, such as illegal dumping, development and pollutants, continue to be a harsh reality. Buccoo Reef, the largest coral reef in Tobago, was made a protected marine park in 1973, but the combined effects of polluting land-based run-off, anchors and reef walking have damaged this impressive system of five reef flats.

FACING PAGE
Blue-crowned motmot

ABOVE: Dolphin-watching in the Gulf of Paria

RIGHT: Leatherback turtle nesting on Grande Tacarib

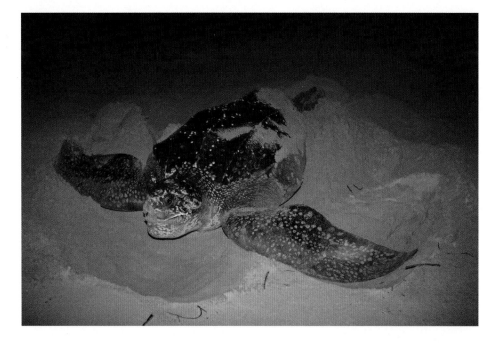

Nature watching

During the nesting season of the endangered leatherback turtle (March to August), the turtle-watching phenomenon can be experienced on three of Trinidad's more accessible turtle-watching beaches: Grand Riviere, Matura and Fishing Pond. The leeward side of Tobago also provides laying grounds for these massive creatures, which can weigh up to 728 kilograms.

From the carnivorous sundew plant of the Aripo Savannah to the sought-after cedros bee orchid of the south-western peninsula, the cave-dwelling oilbird to the endangered manatee, digging into Trinidad and Tobago's ecological treasure trove requires proper time and guidance. A reliable introduction to it all is through the services of certified tour operators, such as those registered with the Trinidad and Tobago Incoming Tour Operators Association. Through such guides, the tourism experience – whether eco, cultural or other – is guaranteed to be a unique one.

As Mother Nature parades her 'bands' throughout the year, more emphasis must be placed on her protection. Serious national discourse, greater governmental support, stronger environmental laws and public education in conservation awareness are steps toward ensuring that the twin-island republic of Trinidad and Tobago nurtures an environment left to be enjoyed for generations to come. ■

CLOCKWISE FROM MAIN PICTURE
Pink hibiscus; green tree frog; blue morpho butterfly; white-necked jacabin; green honeycreeper; purple honeycreeper

In training for the future

DENZIL MOHAMMED

Education in Trinidad and Tobago has always been a source of pride. Its brightest sons of the soil have become renowned scholars in almost every academic field. In the early 1900s, for instance, medical research pioneer Dr Lennox Pawan isolated the virus transmitted by bats that causes rabies in humans. Trinidad and Tobago's first Prime Minister, Dr Eric Williams, was one of the world's foremost historians. His seminal work, *Capitalism and Slavery*, is a superlative text on New World history. In 2001, Sir V.S. Naipaul was awarded the Nobel Prize for Literature for a body of work spanning nearly fifty years.

Today, a strong academic tradition endures. Trinidad and Tobago enjoys a booming economy, driven by the energy sector – oil, natural gas and methanol. Simultaneously, schools at every level have expanded and are continually transforming their curricula to meet worldwide competitiveness and standards. Most recently, a proliferation of tertiary-level institutions have been established, tailored to satisfy the increasing demands of the employment market.

Free tertiary

When Trinidad and Tobago gained Independence from Britain in 1962, the then Prime Minister, Dr Eric Williams, charged the government with guaranteeing free, universal primary education. While approximately 86 percent of children are enrolled in pre-primary schools, primary school enrolment in 2004 was at 92 percent. The bulk of national budget allocations in education typically fall into the primary level sector.

The ambition to educate all heightened in the mid-1990s as the government sought to make secondary education compulsory. New schools were constructed, particularly in rural areas, and existing buildings were expanded to facilitate this objective. The Common Entrance Examination, which preceded entry to secondary school, was discontinued and replaced by the Secondary Entrance Assessment System: a progressive evaluation of students' development that would better ensure continued academic growth. There is now a 97 percent transition rate from primary to secondary school, one of the highest in the world.

Secondary schools offer students opportunities in diverse subject areas, with an emphasis on foreign languages, and natural and social sciences. The number of technical and vocational courses taught in schools has also increased.

In the past decade, however, the thrust of Trinidad and Tobago's education system has been directed at the tertiary level. The St Augustine campus has undertaken massive expansion of infrastructure, facilities, student accommodation, staff and degree programmes towards a target student population of 16,000 by September 2007. There are now more than twenty private and government-run tertiary-level schools across the country, including the new University of Trinidad and Tobago (UTT). In 2004, the government decided to pick up the tab of students' tuition fees, making tertiary education more widely accessible to the qualified.

FACING PAGE: The primary school sector receives the bulk of national budget allocations for education

Photo: Stephen Broadbridge

The University of the West Indies (UWI) and the Eric Williams Medical Sciences Complex at Mount Hope already comprises some seventy buildings that facilitate new undergraduate and postgraduate degree programmes in such diverse fields as film, international relations, geo-sciences, medical sciences and law. It also boasts of being the largest wireless organisation in Trinidad and Tobago, and has even been approached by Microsoft Caribbean as its preferred partner to provide support to other educational institutions throughout the region.

There is a strong correlation between the number of people who have access to tertiary education and the competitiveness of a country. The expansion of the UWI has been complemented by a proliferation of private tertiary education institutions which are affiliated with foreign-based universities such as New Brunswick, London and Leicester.

Private schooling

Specialising, first, in law and business administration and, more recently, in information technology, communications and energy, the popularity of private schools has grown dramatically as the preferred place of learning for many people. Through accelerated programmes that factor in work experiences, prospective students lacking the traditional entry qualifications can gain admission to pursue certificates, associate degrees and master's programmes. Class schedules cater especially for working individuals, and online libraries and tutorials enhance their appeal. Certain major government initiatives have spearheaded development in the teaching and training of skills designed specifically to meet the demands of the burgeoning energy sector.

The Royal Bank of Trinidad and Tobago's Institute of Business and Technology (Roytec), traditionally the place where potential bankers begin after five years of secondary education, formed an alliance with the University of New Brunswick in Canada and now offers courses ranging from journalism to nursing. A college of nursing has also been established by the government, and the National Institute of Higher Education, Research, Science and Technology (NIHERST) operates colleges of health sciences, nursing, languages and information technology.

In 2000, the College of Science, Technology and Applied Arts of Trinidad and Tobago (COSTAATT) opened its doors at decentralised campuses across the country. It was the first national community college in Trinidad and Tobago and brought several existing tertiary-level institutions under one umbrella. It is a 'second-chance' school. It caters for citizens of any age who lack university entry requirements, and also makes it possible for students to begin studies at age sixteen and graduate with an associate degree by age twenty. COSTAATT's curricula are closely linked to the market economy and adapts intelligently to the energy industry and the business community. In this regard, there is high private sector involvement, and students gain credits for work experience. More

Lakshmi Girls' College in
St Augustine
Photo: Kris Rampersad

Secondary schools offer students opportunities in diverse subject areas, with an emphasis on foreign languages and natural and social sciences
Photo: Kris Rampersad

importantly, though, UTT's co-operative approach to education combines institutional learning with relevant practical experience in the workplace. Its decentralised campuses are located on the very sites on which the curricula are based to ensure that educational strategy, teaching content and laboratory facilities closely simulate the actual workplace. These sites include the Point Lisas Industrial Estate in Couva (process and utilities programmes, telecommunications and engineering) and Chaguaramas in Trinidad's north-western peninsula (maritime studies).

The University of Trinidad and Tobago, therefore, is explicitly focused on ensuring that students are prepared for the industrial and energy workplace, that their entrepreneurial capacities are enhanced, and that the labour demands of the energy sector are met. Semesters alternate between on-campus teaching and practical application in industry so that students are in continuous professional contact, can focus on career direction and options, and can refine their interpersonal and communication skills.

Higher level

And yet, despite this concentration on the energy sector and university education, Trinidad and Tobago has never neglected those who may not choose traditional career paths. There are more than fifteen technical and vocational schools throughout the country which schools reinforce and refine skills taught in secondary schools in non-traditional, niche areas as well as technical fields with an emphasis on training.

The National On-The-Job Training programme operates in six-month cycles through the Ministry of Science, Technology and Tertiary Education for people aged sixteen to thirty who are graduates of secondary, technical or vocational schools. The Youth Training and Employment Partnership Programme (YTEPP) is a widely successful enterprise that produces 8,000 graduates annually.

These are but a few of the training opportunities offered to citizens. There is, in fact, a high level of training in Trinidad and Tobago that ensures a ready reserve of local labour equipped to meet the challenges posed by the dynamic and prospering sectors of the economy. The government has taken these critical, forward-thinking initiatives to guarantee that its workforce is highly skilled, progressive and adaptable in order to meet its objective of 'developed nation' status by the year 2020. ∎

Better health care for all

SITA BRIDGEMOHAN

The Ministry of Health has overall responsibility for health care in Trinidad and Tobago and is generally responsible for policy, while five Regional Health Authorities (RHA) provide health care services at primary and secondary public health facilities in the respective regions. The RHAs deliver primary health care – maternal and child health, immunisation, chronic disease and dental clinics with primary care physicians, nurses and pharmacists – through more than a 100 health centres. These clinics offer daily outpatient services and visits with medical specialists. Public health nurses are also available to make house calls and visit schools.

Secondary care is provided by the hospitals in each of the regions including the Port of Spain General Hospital (the country's largest), located in the capital, and the San Fernando General Hospital, located in the island's second largest city and industrial capital. These two hospitals also provide tertiary health services along with the Eric Williams Medical Sciences Complex, which is also a teaching hospital for the Faculty of Medical Sciences at the University of the West Indies.

Most specialists and medical practitioners in Trinidad and Tobago are trained in the United Kingdom and the United States. A recent annual government scholarship programme for doctors at the St George's University in Grenada, is expected to provide additional trained medical doctors to complement the quota originating from the Faculty of Medical Sciences at UWI. The University of the West Indies has also established a Bachelor of Science Nursing Degree in Advance Nursing Practice.

Apart from the primary, secondary and tertiary health care institutions, other specialised facilities include St Ann's Hospital for psychiatric care, Caura Hospital for cardiology and pathology services, and St James Infirmary for geriatric, oncological, and physical therapeutic care.

SECTOR REFORM

Under a Health Sector Reform Programme (HSRP), an Emergency Health System serves the islands along with several other projects with the aim of delivering better health care service to all residents. A number of health care programmes have been established under this programme including a special elective

Located in the capital, Port of Spain General Hospital is the country's largest hospital
Photo: Stephen Broadbridge

surgery programme to reduce the waiting lists at hospitals for cataract, hernia and fibroids operations and a subsidised surgery programme for angiograms, angioplasty and open-heart surgery.

One of the on-going initiatives under the HSRP is the establishment of a modern hospital in Tobago to replace the Tobago Regional Hospital in Scarborough. Under the HSRP, the Ministry and the RHAs can sub-contract services from the private sector, research organisations, training institutions and non-governmental organisations for equipment maintenance and supplies as well as for clinical services from independent physicians and others.

Health care is also provided through the private sector (for a fee) by family practitioners and specialists. These doctors generally also work in the public sector. Several private medical centres also provide excellent health care, also for a fee.

AIDS TREATMENT

Among the most important initiatives of the HSRP is the launch of a national, five-year HIV/AIDS plan focusing on prevention, treatment, care and support. Launched in September 2004, the HIV/AIDS National Strategic Plan includes testing, as well as a programme for voluntary counselling and testing for HIV/AIDS. Specifically, the Tobago AIDS Clinic has recorded significant success in treatment which includes use of anti-retroviral drugs as well as counselling to deal with the disease as well as to effect lifestyle changes. But perhaps the most significant development in the battle against HIV/AIDS has been the government's anti-retroviral programme which offers free AIDS drugs to patients who sign up for the programme. Trinidad and Tobago is the only country in the region to offer this facility.

The National HIV/AIDS Strategic Plan also identifies the reduction in stigma and discrimination against people living with HIV/AIDS as one of the key objectives in the response to the epidemic. Peer education and counselling programmes, aimed at both youths and parents, complement the efforts to encourage religious groups, the private sector and non-governmental organisations to become involved in the national AIDS programme.

FREE ACCESS

One of the more significant achievements in public health care in Trinidad and Tobago is the implementation of a Chronic Disease Assistance Programme (CDAP). Under CDAP, a range of medications for chronic diseases such as hypertension and heart disease are now available free to the public from selected pharmacies across the nation. Another benchmark in public health care is the free public access, upon referral from other public health institutions, to the Eric Williams Medical Sciences Complex.

Photo: Shirley Bahadur

Liberalised stream of voices across the media

DENZIL MOHAMMED

Since the opening up of the airwaves in 1991, the media industry in Trinidad and Tobago has mushroomed. In just twenty years, the number of television stations grew from one to eight, and radio stations burgeoned from four to thirty-four. Virtually every niche market is now targeted – from inner-city youth to the politically inclined – and new choices in programming and print are opening up annually.

The advent of cable television and the de-monopolisation of the telecommunications industry have seen an exponential escalation in cell phone use, information dissemination and Internet access, bringing citizens in closer communication.

Between Independence in 1962 and the early 1990s, TV and radio were all state-owned. There was some attempt to develop programmes about local culture. Vanguard programmes from that era have left indelible impressions on the cultural landscape. Shows such as 'Calabash Alley', a grassroots soap opera where many local actors got started, and 'Cross Country', an in-depth travel documentary, linger endearingly in the minds of 'Trinbagonians', both here and abroad.

However, the limitations of the state monopoly restricted information access to world news and events, pop culture and to local niche activities. It also inhibited the voice of the people, which the privately-owned newspapers alone could not adequately address. Consequently, by the time the Trinidad and Tobago government liberalised broadcast programming in 1991, a stream of new TV and radio stations flooded the market. Immediately, the effect was heard on the radio frequencies.

Niche markets

From four stations that concentrated on culture, religion and news, thirty-four stations gradually found places on the radio dial and ushered a boom in the entertainment industry. The inner-city beats of 96.1 WEFM led a surge of hip-hop, R&B, reggae and dancehall on the airwaves, while soca star, Neil "Iwer" George's 91.9 FM 'Trini Bashment' pounds the Caribbean rhythms.

Indian culture is espoused on Radio 90.5 FM and Sangeet 106.5 FM, 103FM, to name a few. These stations have given voice to Indian-Trinidadians and they host popular family days, kite-flying competitions, curry duck limes, and cultural shows annually, institutionalising them in the country.

American popular culture has its home on stations such as The Mix 95.1 FM and Hott 93.5 FM, while the swelling mature audience tunes in to Music Radio 97 and others.

Of growing importance, however, is the civic journalism practised by radio stations such as Power 102 FM and 95.5 FM, in addition to the Indian cultural stations and community radio such as Radio Tambrin. These stations have well-established talk shows and, like US network programmes such as 'Meet the Press', regularly feature political, business and community leaders for public interaction. There are also niches created for sports programming in 100.7 FM, for religion, for local music, and for pop.

Cable TV outbreak

Radio isn't the only medium that has flourished in the past two decades. Cable television is available across both islands and offers a basic package of about seventy channels at relatively low-cost. Among the eight television stations, there are six local cable channels that provide news, entertainment (the BET-style Synergy TV headed by young soca superstar Machel Montano) and religious programming (Islamic Broadcast Network). Gayelle TV, in particular, brings one back to the olden days of cultural programming and local films. Government-owned stations include CNMG and NCC TV.

In 2006, the Cable Company of Trinidad and Tobago announced the introduction of Flow, a bundled cable/Internet/phone service, which is already servicing East Trinidad. Satellite television through DirecTV is also a popular choice across demographic demarcations. Caribbean Communications Network (CCN) launched TV6 in 1991 with a salvo of modern American sitcoms and news reporting. It was the sister station to the *Trinidad Express* newspaper, established in the 1960s.

Image revamp

Indeed, newspapers in Trinidad and Tobago have undergone significant changes in the past decade. *Newsday*, established in the 1993, joined the *Express* to capture the audience that wanted tabloid-styled news. With the new competition, the *Trinidad Guardian*, for ninety years a broadsheet, dramatically changed its image, and reduced its size, to do battle with its new rivals.

With the advent of the Internet and the proliferation of live news television, newspaper circulation worldwide has been in decline. In this regard, local newspapers have given their news coverage an overhaul, stressing more dynamic reporting and more succinct stories for people on the go. They are also dipping into niche markets that have traditionally been the least inclined to buy a newspaper – women and youth – with special supplements and regular features on lifestyle, fashion, entertainment and education.

Local magazines are also tapping into niche markets. In keeping with international trends, publications focus on health and the outdoors (*Sport and Fitness*) and lifestyle and real estate (*Maco*). Others, such as BWIA's successful in-flight magazine, *Caribbean Beat*, concentrate on sport, art and the individual achievements of Caribbean personalities, seeking explicitly to ameliorate the image of the region and discard its stereotypes.

Wireless time

Most of these magazines have Internet editions. Indeed, all of the daily newspapers publish online and some radio stations offer live streaming. Schools across the country, brimming with tech-savvy youngsters, are furnished with computer labs and Internet access. Most local companies, including banks and the service industry, as well as government and parliament, support modern websites.

Wireless Internet access from various Internet Service Providers is gaining in popularity and affordability. The St Augustine campus of the University of the West Indies is the largest wireless organisation in the region, and free wireless Internet access can be found at both the Piarco and Crown Point International airports, restaurants and cafes, shopping malls and hotels.

Cell phones have also proliferated in the past decade. Low rates and new competition in the telecommunications market have prompted a dramatic rise in the number of cell phones in Trinidad and Tobago. As of August 2005, there were 620,000 cell phone subscribers in contrast to 320,000 fixed-line subscribers. With the advent of GSM (Global System for Mobile) and, now, third generation CDMA (Code Division Multiple Access) 2000 wireless technology, the cell phone boom will continue with lower costs, better service and contemporary technology.

Free reign

Despite the media and telecommunications explosion in Trinidad and Tobago, there is little at present to govern or regulate media activity. Protected by constitutional provisions of freedom of speech and of the press, the media is largely a self-regulatory body.

A Broadcast Code has recently been produced with the input of media practitioners and industry stakeholders which seeks, among other things, to ensure more local content is broadcast, that rated programmes are delegated appropriate timeslots and warnings, and that, in this multi-cultural, multi-ethnic and multi-religious society, people's rights are not infringed upon or unduly offended. The talk show phenomenon, in particular, is widely considered to be a potential source of hatred and prejudice and there is advocacy for a code of conduct to ensure all citizens are fairly treated and have the necessary recourse should rights be trampled. By and large, Trinidad and Tobago enjoys a growing dynamism and healthy media environment. ■

Red House is the seat of
the nation's Parliament
Photo: Ian Brierley

Politics of change and reform

SITA BRIDGEMOHAN

Trinidad became a colony of Spain when it was claimed by Christopher Columbus in 1498 on his third voyage to the 'New World'. The Spanish imposed its political systems and religion on the indigenous Amerindian tribes in an attempt to 'civilise' them. Instead, oppression and enslavement, as well as the diseases brought by the Europeans, led to the decimation of most of the Amerindian population.

In 1797, Britain (during its war with Spain) seized Trinidad and claimed it as a British colony. It remained part of Britain's empire until Trinidad and Tobago gained independence in 1962. During its rule, Britain would preside over the abolition of slavery on the island (1834) and the implementation of new systems of labour for the island's European planters – Indian indentureship (1845 to 1917) and Chinese immigration (1848 to 1866).

In 1889, Tobago was annexed to Trinidad when its sugar-based economy collapsed, giving rise to the unitary state of Trinidad and Tobago.

The road to independence

In the first half of the 20th century, the nation's population comprised, largely, of people of African and Indian descent. Since the discovery of oil in 1857, the country's economy had changed from one based upon agriculture to that of a lucrative oil producer. And Britain was still in charge.

However, the rise of social consciousness among the general population led to political unrest and calls for local representation in the running of the nation's affairs. This eventually led to the first elections in Trinidad and Tobago in 1946. In the 1956 elections, the People's National Movement (PNM), led by Dr Eric Williams, emerged on the political scene, winning thirteen of the twenty-four seats being contested in the election. Dr Williams became the country's first prime minister. The party would also win the 1961 elections, setting the stage for gaining independence from Britain the following year.

The PNM ruled for thirty years until it was defeated in 1985. Throughout its period as the ruling party, the PNM faced challenges to its administration with dissident voices calling for social change through the 1970 Black Power uprising and an attempted military coup. The party also presided over the final severing of all political ties with Britain when Trinidad and Tobago became a republic in 1976, exchanging the Queen as head of state, for a president, and a new republican constitution. The prime minister remained as head of government in a parliamentary system of democracy.

Changing guards

In the 1985 elections, a coalition of three political parties defeated the PNM government winning thirty-three of the thirty-six seats. It was a critical time in Trinidad and Tobago's history – the International Monetary Fund (IMF) had called for drastic economic reforms to avert economic collapse, and citizens were called upon to tighten their belts to deal with the austerity measures being implemented.

Dr Eric Williams, above, was Trinidad and Tobago's first prime minister followed by George Chambers, below

PRESIDENTS OF TRINIDAD AND TOBAGO SINCE 1976

George Maxwell Richards
17 March 2003 to present
Arthur N.R. Robinson
19 March 1997 to 17 March 2003
Noor Hassanali
19 March 1987 to 19 March 1997
Ellis Clarke
1 August 1976 to 13 March 1987

PRIME MINISTERS OF TRINIDAD AND TOBAGO SINCE 1956

Patrick Manning
24 December 2001 to present
Basdeo Panday
9 Nov 1995 to 24 Dec 2001
Patrick Manning
17 Dec 1991 to 9 Nov 1995
A.N.R. Robinson
19 Dec 1986 to 17 Dec 1991
George Chambers
30 March 1981 to 18 Dec 1986
Eric Williams
28 October 1956 to 29 March 1981

The NAR ruled for one term and were defeated in 1991 by the PNM. However, after a snap election in 1995, the party was defeated by another coalition. The PNM and the newly created United National Congress (UNC), each won seventeen seats, while the NAR won the two Tobago seats. The UNC and the NAR joined together to form the government led by Basdeo Panday.

The UNC won the next election but held on to government for only a short period before it was deprived of its majority in parliament after three of its members quit. Forced into another election in 2001, the polls produced an historic deadlock of 18 seats each for the UNC and the PNM. It was left to the president to choose the prime minister from the leaders of the two deadlocked parties; he chose the political leader of the PNM, Patrick Manning. Panday, as incumbent, declared this decision unconstitutional and refused to abide by it; parliament was unable to function for nine months. To break this deadlock, new elections were again called in October 2002. In this, the PNM won twenty seats to the UNC's sixteen and remained in government. In 2005, the numbers of parliamentary seats were increased to forty-four.

Towards constitutional reform

With the stalemate of 2001 still a fresh memory in the political consciousness of Trinidad and Tobago, the issue of constitutional reform is seen as an urgent need to meet the demands of an evolving society. Indeed, constitutional reform has been an area of political concern for decades in the country. Now, the government has started the process of reform by laying in Parliament a draft of a new constitution for public discussion. The main element of the draft is a recommendation for the position of an executive president to consolidate and replace the positions of prime minister and president. The executive president will have to face the electorate at the polls first, and be successful, to qualify for nomination as executive president. Then he or she will be elected by members of the House of Representatives in separate elections by secret ballot. The draft also makes recommendations for the post of a vice-president and the office of leader of the opposition.

Parliament would remain a bicameral legislature with the Lower House elected by way of the current 'first past the post' system while the Upper House would be enlarged to include members elected by local government bodies. The judicial system is also targeted for reform with the recommendation being that the Caribbean Court of Justice should replace the Privy Council in London as the country's final court of appeal.

Foreign relations

Independent Trinidad and Tobago has always insisted on an identity as a fully sovereign nation as it forged links and relations with Caribbean and international countries and organisations. Indeed, even pre-independent Trinidad and Tobago sought to establish itself as a nation wanting to, and capable of, making its own decisions. Under Dr Eric

LEFT (l-r)
Former president, A.N.R. Robinson and former prime minister, Basdeo Panday
Photos: S Bahadur

Opening of Parliament
Photo: Shirley Bahadur

President George Maxwell Richards
(above) and Prime Minister Patrick
Manning
Photos: Shirley Bahadur

Williams, the country won the right to sit as a sovereign member with the United States and Britain at the 1960 conference that decided the fate of the US base at Chaguaramas. But in 1962 he pulled out of the West Indies Federation in the interest of securing the economic well-being of Trinidad and Tobago.

With its economy fuelled by oil, Trinidad and Tobago continued to foster good relations with its regional neighbours. It was a founding member of the Caribbean Free Trade Association (Carifta) and is a member of the successor organisation, Caricom, which was established in 1973. It represents the largest market in Caricom, responsible for about eighty percent of trade, while Caricom represents its second largest export market after the US.

Regional relations have extended to the provision of financial aid for development, through grants to the Caribbean Development Bank and government-to-government loans and in recent times have included an initiative for a natural gas pipeline project to supply natural gas to certain Caribbean countries.

Among regional integration initiatives, the implementation the Caribbean Single Market and Economy (CSME) in January 2006 is expected to increase trade among the participating countries and also facilitate the movement of Caribbean citizens throughout the region.

In 1995, Trinidad and Tobago hosted the inaugural meeting of the Association of Caribbean States (ACS), a thirty-five-member grouping which seeks to further economic progress and integration among its members. The ACS headquarters are located in Port of Spain.

Trinidad and Tobago also plays an active role in international organisations such as the United Nations which it joined in 1962, the same year it became a member of the Commonwealth of Nations. In March 1967, it became the first Commonwealth Caribbean member of the Organisation of American States (OAS), signing on soon after to the Inter-American Treaty of Reciprocal Assistance (Rio Treaty) of 1947 and becoming a part of the inter-American regional security mechanism under the framework of the UN Charter.

Trinidad and Tobago is also a member-state of the International Criminal Court, without a Bilateral Immunity Agreement of protection for the US military.

In terms of its relations with Britain, Trinidad and Tobago retains the Judicial Committee of the Privy Council in London as its highest court of appeal. ■

Another boom time for the economy

LOUIS ARAUJO

Some would say that Trinidad and Tobago has been here before. Buoyed by high energy prices, the nation's economy is experiencing a boom and along with that come the benefits and challenges of a country trying to maximize the revenues from a natural resource.

While there are similarities between the current boom and the period of high energy prices in the late 1970s, some economists point out that the differences are as important as the similarities. Chief among those is the fact that the Trinidad and Tobago economy is now based primarily on natural gas which, in terms of price, is not as volatile as oil. Gas, with its long-term contracts, has allowed the government to plan with more certainty about future revenues.

The current wave of spending is being generated, mainly, by the government. State spending and high energy revenues have pushed growth from 4.2 percent in 2001 to over seven percent projected for 2006. At the same time, unemployment has decreased from thirteen percent in 1999 to around six percent. With the fast-paced growth and falling unemployment, economists are now suggesting that the economy is nearing capacity, as can be seen in the labour shortages that are cropping up outside of the construction and state sectors.

The government is faced with the challenge of using energy revenues to develop infrastructure that has been lacking. Infrastructure development goes hand-in-hand with general national development and the government has identified transportation, housing and public sector office space as the key areas. At the same time, the capital, Port of Spain, is being transformed with the Waterfront Development Project that will see the expansion of large-scale conference facilities.

RIGHT: BP processing plant at Point Galeota in Trinidad

Photo: Stephen Broadbridge

Intellectual capital

Development is also taking place at the level of intellectual capital. A shift in the approach to education is taking place, with the government concentrating not only on its traditional strength – the energy sector – but also innovation and entrepreneurship in others sectors, including the manufacturing sector.

The change is being driven by the establishment of the University of Trinidad and Tobago (UTT) which is focusing on producing industry-ready graduates in a number of fields. The difference between UTT and the University of the West Indies is its heavy emphasis on practical experience and entrepreneurship, a combination that should produce professionals who can create their own niche in industries. The university is being led by Professor Ken Julien, the man responsible for the development of Trinidad and Tobago's natural gas industry and who has been an integral part of shaping this country's path during its current oil and gas boom. Professor Julien is also a key figure at the University of the West Indies, and he has been joined by a number of Trinidad and Tobago nationals who are based overseas.

Another key component of the development of innovation and industry is the development of an industrial park in east Trinidad. The Tamana eTecK Park, as it will be named, is designed to attract companies from a variety of industries and will provide a base for the growth of locally-driven research and development. The development of the eTecK Park will be accompanied by the establishment of new towns surrounding the park itself.

Roads

A part of infrastructure development has been widening the roads that lead into the capital city. Another sign of Trinidad and Tobago's burgeoning economy has unfortunately been the added congestion on the nation's roadways, a testament to an increase in the number of cars on the road as well as the growth in business.

The road system is being tackled from two fronts. The first is to facilitate access into Port of Spain. That includes widening the highways leading into the capital and at least one major road within the capital itself. There are also plans to extend the highway system further south than it now reaches to facilitate development of south Trinidad. One of the consequences of increased activity in the petrochemical sector has been the need to find more space to locate new plants. Point Lisas, home of Trinidad and Tobago's

FACING PAGE
Processing sea freight at
the docks in Port of Spain
Photo: Stephen Broadbridge

RIGHT: Evolving TecKnologies and Enterprise Development Company Limited (eTecK) is a special purpose state enterprise operating under the aegis of the Ministry of Trade and Industry. eTecK is responsible for developing the light industrial parks in Trinidad and Tobago by encouraging diversification of the country's non-energy and downstream from energy production and export bases, exploring niche areas of investment for local and foreign companies, as well as providing infrastructural support by development of eTecK Parks throughout Trinidad and Tobago. eTecK is also responsible for country branding and investment promotion.

ABOVE: The Suez Matthew loading the 1000th LNG cargo (in October 2006) produced by the Atlantic LNG facility at Point Fortin (top). This ship also transported the first LNG cargo produced by Trinidad and Tobago in 1999. Through its supply contracts with Atlantic, Suez LNG has enabled locally-produced natural gas to access the US market.

FACING PAGE
Construction in Port of Spain

Photo: Stephen Broadbridge

petrochemical sector, is located in central Trinidad but has reached the limit for expansion. To counter that, the government plans to develop a number of industrial parks along the south-west coast along with a system of ports to facilitate the export of petrochemicals and other commodities such as aluminium products.

The second front for improvement of the road system is the construction of a rapid rail project which will connect east and west Trinidad. Estimated to cost about $15 billion, the scheme should begin construction in 2007.

Utilities

Along with the road infrastructure, there are also plans to upgrade the electricity and water systems. Neither sector has seen a major upgrade, and the time is now right to catch up to present needs and set in place plans for the future.

The government is seeking to pump $27 billion into the Water and Sewerage Authority to improve supply. That would include mainly the replacement and upgrade of transmission lines. Power generation is also being expanded to cater for the new industries being proposed.

Diversification

About a century since the oil well was drilled in Trinidad and Tobago, today's economy remains driven primarily by oil and gas, a fact that leads the country to be open to the ebb and flow of international prices and markets. While the energy sector has remained the mainstay, the country has developed in other areas as well but the correlation to the energy sector remains. During the recession that followed the last boom in the 1980s, Trinidad and Tobago's manufacturing sector took the lead, encouraged by the government to make a mark, first at home, then throughout the region and the world.

Faced with low oil prices and the subsequent decline in revenue in the early 1980s, the government turned its attention to the manufacturing sector as a means of diversifying away from energy. It was not an easy road for manufacturers at the time since they had to overcome severe foreign exchange crunches to build an industry from scratch. From those early days, however, Trinidad and Tobago's manufacturing sector has grown to

Port of Spain
overlooking the
Gulf of Paria
Photo: S Broadbridge

become a powerhouse in the region, with firms already making a footprint in Latin America and further afield in Europe and beyond. Trinidad and Tobago's open, competitive policy has meant that local goods compete with foreign competitors on local shelves but they have been able to hold their own in terms of price and quality.

Local companies have developed a number of markets, from food and beverage to household products. The Caribbean Common Market (Caricom) remains this country's major trading partner, followed by the United States. Local firms have built on the advantages that Trinidad and Tobago has to offer – mainly low energy costs – and their dominance of regional trade has also led this country to take the lead in international trade negotiations. Strong negotiation teams have allowed Trinidad and Tobago and Caricom to carve out favourable trade deals with their Latin American neighbours. To support those trade pacts, Parliament recently enhanced fair trading legislation to ensure that all firms – local and foreign – compete evenly in the local market.

The manufacturing sector contributes about 4.9 percent to the economy, but it is in employment that its presence is felt, representing ten percent of all jobs in 2004. Having established itself during the period of low energy prices, the manufacturing sector now finds itself, in some ways, competing with the energy sector for resources now that the tables have turned. There is some cause for concern as the labour market is stretched by new projects in the construction sector and state-run programmes. The government, however, is trying to address this imbalance by increasing opportunities for training and on-the-job training, a move that should strengthen the links between the manufacturing sector and the labour market.

In the shadow of Nicholas Tower, home to the Trinidad and Tobago Stock Exchange, Independence Square in Port of Spain is home to a diverse range of businesses
Photo: S Broadbridge

ABOVE: Celebrating fifteen years since opening its doors in Trinidad and Tobago, Courts has grown to be a familiar landmark in many towns throughout the country. With its nineteen stores, this retailer of furniture, appliances and electronics has made a remarkable impact on its sector. The company is best known for its support of the local furniture manufacturing industry, its aggressive pricing strategies and strong promotional background. A member of the Courts International Group, this company is part of an eleven-strong Caribbean presence with over 2000 associates to serve its customers.

FACING PAGE
Selling peppers at Chaguanas market
Photo: Stephen Broadbridge

Financial Sector

Trinidad and Tobago's financial sector has grown hand-in-hand with the economy, mirroring, in many respects, the rise of the manufacturing sector. The financial sector has also been pushed along by the country's buoyant economy. Some have estimated the amount of money available for investment at around US$1 billion. Trinidad and Tobago's aim is to be the financial capital of the region, an aim that is bolstered by the fact that Trinidad and Tobago is the site for both regional governments and firms to raise capital, pushed by the work of local merchant banks. Regional bond issues, for example, reached just over $690 million in 2004.

That effort has been helped with the establishment of the Caribbean Credit Rating Agency (CariCRIS) which recently started to rate local and regional institutions. CariCRIS will go a long way towards giving investors an understanding of the risks involved in issues and institutions that are not rated by international agencies.

As another example of the size of Trinidad and Tobago's financial market, the local mutual funds industry grew by 22.7 percent to $22.9 billion by the end of 2004 with annualised yields on investment averaging over 26 percent. Between 31 December 2002 and 30 November 2005, the number of registered domestic funds actively traded grew by around 173 percent, from fifteen funds to 41.

One of the major issues right now is whether the financial market is big enough to invest directly in the energy sector projects. While the general feeling is that the local sector cannot bear the brunt of energy sector investment, debate now continues around what type of instruments would best allow local investors to participate on a smaller scale. That would allow them to reap some of the benefits of the energy sector without being exposed to too much of the risk involved.

Agriculture

Once the mainstay of Trinidad's economy – through sugar and then cocoa – agriculture has again been pushed into the forefront as the country grapples with sharply increasing food prices. As a sector, agriculture has consistently been on the decline since the end of the cocoa industry at the beginning of the 1900s. Sugar, although a main ingredient in Trinidad and Tobago's powerful beverage industry, was heavily subsidized by the government; and the company responsible for sugar production, Caroni (1975) Ltd, was closed in 2003.

There is already a fair amount of fresh produce export to neighbouring islands as well as the US.

With the closure of Caroni, new land has been opened-up for the cultivation of other crops. Caroni's land and Trinidad's traditional food-baskets, are now being seen as key components in the drive to increase agricultural production and, ultimately, to keep prices of fresh produce at bay.

Future forecast

Although Trinidad and Tobago has passed through booms before, it is difficult to chart the country's course from here since the country today is, in many respects, far different from the country of twenty years ago. What is clear is that Trinidad and Tobago will continue to find its niche in financial services as the local capital market develops. There will also be scope for continued expansion of manufactured goods, especially high-end products. What is not clear, however, is how much of a role these sectors will play – as opposed to the energy sector – in twenty years. Diversification away from oil and gas remains the main goal, but where that goal will lead remains to be seen. ■

Towards bloc trading

LOUIS ARAUJO

Trinidad and Tobago's energy industry drives its trade balances. Oil, natural gas and other products like lubricants account for about seventy percent of all exports. Petrochemicals accounted for about sixteen percent and manufacturing about six percent.

While Trinidad and Tobago's manufacturing exports only account for about six percent, it remains a dominant force in the region for non-energy goods, a role that began after the oil slump in the early 1980s. That position has given the country the opportunity to take the lead in regional and international trade arrangements.

The country's trade with Caricom neighbours is also driven by petrochemical products. According to figures from the Central Statistical Office, between January and November 2005, Trinidad and Tobago exported $10 billion worth of goods, accounting for about 21 percent of exports. During that period imports from the region were valued at $650 million.

But Caricom itself is evolving. The region is moving ahead with its Caricom Single Market and Economy that will see a further deepening of the ties between members. The economic bloc that was built mainly around goods is now tackling trade in services, looking at areas like financial services. The region took another step on 1 January 2006 with the introduction of the free movement of labour. That step began with the major players with Caricom, while the Organisation of Eastern Caribbean States joined later in 2006.

The region is also moving towards closer economic union, a move that could see a European Union-styled interaction on issues like inflation and a common currency. That, though, is still some way off.

The world is evolving into economic blocs and the region is no exception. The Caribbean countries have been forced to come together to tighten its trade ties among themselves and develop relationships as a group with other regions.

The make-up of Caricom dictates that no one country can negotiate on its own. Trinidad and Tobago started negotiations with Costa Rica on a free trade deal but it was soon expanded to include the rest of Caricom. Those negotiations also set the stage for Trinidad and Tobago's role within Caricom trade. The Caricom/Costa Rica Free Trade Agreement includes very open trade between Costa Rica and Trinidad and Tobago but includes special terms for other Caricom neighbours, limiting access by Costa Rica.

Another important trade agreement is the one that Caricom has negotiated with the Dominican Republic. The trade balance between Trinidad and Tobago and the Dominican Republic is heavily in Trinidad and Tobago's favour, mainly due to LNG exports, but there is also trade in some manufactured goods. The two sides have now begun talks on the services part of the agreement.

Bilateral free trade deals, like the Costa Rica deal, are becoming more important after the failure of the Free Trade Area of the Americas. The FTAA would have seen a hemisphere-wide trade bloc but countries are now using FTAA as a base to negotiate country-to-country deals.

Caricom's next challenge is to clinch a free trade deal with the United States. Trade with that country is now influenced by the Caribbean Basin Initiative (CBI) that allows duty free entry for certain goods from the Caribbean. The CBI, a one-way trade deal, is coming to an end and needs to be replaced with a reciprocal trade deal that is more along the line of World Trade Organisation rules.

The US accounted for about fifty percent of Trinidad and Tobago's exports in 2005, again, driven mainly by natural gas exports, but Trinidad and Tobago does export manufactured goods under the CBI. The thinking is that the deal should not take long to finalise once talks start.

Caricom as a region has also begun talks with the EU to hammer out new Economic Partnership Agreements, as they are called. These EPAs will dictate a new relationship between the two sides that moves away from European subsidization of goods like sugar and bananas. They will focus more on development assistance. For Trinidad and Tobago, which has drastically reduced its sugar industry, the EPAs will be important in forming how services are exported between the two countries. That means taking a look at how professionals like engineers from the EU, for example, can work in the region and vice versa.

Cutting sugar cane: Economic Partnership Agreements will dictate a new relationship between Caricom and the European Union that moves away from European subsidization of goods like sugar

Photo: Shirley Bahadur

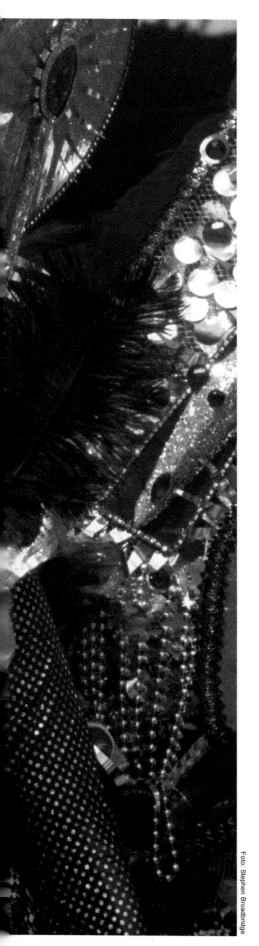

Foto: Stephen Broadbridge

Trinidad und Tobago: Ein einzigartiges karibisches Erlebnis

In einem Gebiet, das ohnehin für seine natürliche Schönheit und vielfältige Kultur bekannt ist, stechen die beiden Inseln der Republik Trinidad und Tobago (5.128 km²) trotzdem hervor. Im Unterschied zu den Vulkan- oder Kalkstein- und Korallenformationen im Norden gleicht die Geologie auf diesen, den südlichsten Außenposten der Kleinen Antillen eher der des südamerikanischen Festlands, mit welchem sie einst verbunden waren. Die Gebirgskette „Northern Range" auf Trinidad war eine Verlängerung der Anden. Diese südamerikanische Herkunft erklärt die reiche Flora und Fauna beider Inseln, wie man sie in ihrer Vielfalt auf keiner anderen Karibikinsel wieder findet.

Doch die Einzigartigkeit von Trinidad und Tobago beschränkt sich nicht nur auf Naturschätze wie den Asphaltsee „Pitch Lake" in Trinidad oder Tobagos „Central Forest Reserve", dem ältesten Regenwaldschutzgebiet der westlichen Hemisphäre. Hauptsächlich aufgrund seiner Historie gibt es in Trinidad heute eine der internationalsten und multikulturellsten Gesellschaften der Welt, während in Tobago stolz eine der stärksten afrikanischen Kulturen der Karibik im Zeitalter des Internet fortbesteht.

Ursprünglich wurde Trinidad von amerindianischen Stämmen aus dem Nordwesten Südamerikas besiedelt, die es "Iere" (Land des Kolibris) nannten, doch bekam es seinen heutigen Namen von Kolumbus, der 1498 drei Hügel an der südlichen Küste aufragen sah. Tobago ist die amerindianische Bezeichnung für Tabak und erinnert somit an eine weitere europäische Obsession, wie auch Gold und Zucker, die die Geschichte der Inseln während der Kolonialzeit prägten.

Während die Niederländer, Letten, Franzosen und Engländer um Tobago kämpften, um den Traum zu realisieren, „so reich wie ein Plantagenbesitzer von Tobago" zu werden, siechte Trinidad bis Ende des 18. Jahrhunderts als Provinz des spanischen Kolonialreichs dahin. Erst der Aufruf der spanischen Krone nach römisch-katholischen Siedlern hatte zur Folge, dass sich französische Plantagenbesitzer mit ihren afrikanischen Sklaven aus Martinique, Grenada und Haiti niederließen.

Dies war der Anfang des modernen Trinidad. Die Franzosen rodeten die Wälder für Plantagen und führten den Karneval und die kreolische Lebensfreude ein, welche später, zusammen mit Einflüssen der verschiedenen Kulturen, aus denen die Sklaven stammten, das Grundgestein für die „Trini"-Kultur bilden sollte. Als die Briten 1797 landeten, fanden sie eine Kolonie vor, die französisch-kreolisch sprach und dem spanischen Recht unterlag. Nach der Abschaffung der Sklaverei 1838 wurde Trinidad noch multikultureller: aus China, Indien und Madeira importierte Arbeitsverpflichtete, von der britischen Navy auf See freigelassene afrikanische Sklaven sowie Krämer aus dem Nahen Osten trugen dazu bei, eine weltweit einzigartige gemischte, kreative und harmonische Gesellschaft zu schaffen. Hier leben Christen, Hindus und Muslime Seite an Seite zusammen und verleihen dem „trinbagoischen" Ausspruch „All a wee is one" („Wir alle sind eins") Bedeutung.

Karneval, Calypso und Steelpans sind nur einige der einzigartigen Besonderheiten dieser Inseln – Errungenschaften, die so gar nicht im Verhältnis zu ihrer eigentlichen Größe stehen. Mit dem Ausdruck ‚Callaloo' (einer reichhaltigen Suppe aus vielen verschiedenen Zutaten) lässt sich Trinidads multikulturelle Gesellschaft am ehesten beschreiben. Diese Mischung zeigt sich im originellen Gebrauch der Sprache, der Architektur (von den „Magnificent Seven" des „Queen's Park Savannah" bis hin zu den im ganzen Land verbreiteten Hindu-Tempeln und Moscheen) sowie der Küche des Landes, die ihren Ursprung in Afrika, Indien und China hat.

Trinidad, wie auch seine kleinere Schwesterinsel, ist wahrlich gesegnet. Südlich der verheerenden Hurrikanzone gelegen, verfügt diese Oase über Energieressourcen (Erdöl- und –gas sowie die daraus resultierende petrochemische Industrie), durch die sie zum finanziellen, kommerziellen und industriellen Zentrum der Ostkaribik sowie zur unangefochtenen Party-Hauptstadt der Gegend wurde. Die Hauptstadt Port of Spain vereint Kolonialgeschichte mit allen Vorteilen und dem Lifestyle einer Metropole des 21. Jahrhunderts. Moderne Sehenswürdigkeiten wie die neue Nationalbibliothek oder die Wolkenkratzer auf der Brian Lara Promenade am Independence Square ergänzen sich wunderschön mit der historischen Architektur des „Red House", dem Parlamentsgebäude, oder den kompliziert gearbeiteten Holzhäusern der Vorstädte. Die Drive-In Einkaufszentren, Wohnanlagen und Luxusapartments entlang der Küste der westlichen Halbinsel sind Beweis für Trinidads Bereitschaft, die Zukunft mit offenen Armen zu begrüßen.

Doch eines der vielen Paradoxe Trinidads ist, dass man nur eine kurze Autofahrt von der geschäftigen Hauptstadt entfernt auf die Vergangenheit trifft: ländliche indische Dörfer, in denen Hindu-Gebetsfahnen im Wind flattern, und der Anblick eines mit Zuckerrohr beladenen Ochsenfuhrwerks genauso vertraut ist wie der eines Kaimanen, der die Straße entlang watschelt.

Das im Süden des Landes gelegene San Fernando ist die zweitgrößte Stadt Trinidads und verdankt einen Großteil seiner Bedeutung den nahe gelegenen Ölfeldern sowohl an Land als auch im Meer. Chaguanas in der Mitte des Landes ist die am schnellsten wachsende Stadt der Insel, Point Fortin eine weitere „Öl-Siedlung" und das östliche Arima eine alte Kakaostadt, in deren Stadtteil Santa Rosa die Nachfahren der ursprünglichen karibischen Inselbewohner leben.

Von den insgesamt 1,3 Mio. Einwohnern der Republik sind nur 50.000 Tobagoer, meist afrikanischer Herkunft. Afrikanische Folklore und die afrikanischen Rhythmen der Tambrin-Musik bestehen in Hügeldörfern wie Moriah und Whim fort und werden beim jährlichen Heritage Festival präsentiert. Scarborough ist die einzige größere Stadt und die ‚Tranquil Isle' (‚Besinnliche Insel') ist zu Recht stolz auf ihren sehr viel langsameren Lifestyle. Ein guter Rat für alle Besucher: in Trinidad feiern und in Tobago ausspannen. Mit seinen unberührten Stränden und den besten Tauchgebieten in der Ostkaribik hat Tobago, im Gegensatz zu Inseln mit abgeschirmten All-Inclusive-Ferienorten und Massentourismus, einen Nischenmarkt für sanften Öko-Tourismus entwickelt.

Obschon Trinidad durch den Karneval weltweit bekannt ist, stand es erst kürzlich mit seiner Fußballnationalmannschaft, den „Soca Warriors", auf der Weltbühne, als diese eine wahrlich temperamentvolle Vorstellung bei der Fußballweltmeisterschaft in Deutschland darboten. Der tobagoische Kapitän Dwight Yorke sowie Russell Latapy von Trinidad sind beide Veteranen der Mannschaft von 1989 und waren unter den ersten Spielern der Republik, die heute Profi-Fußball in Europa, Amerika, Japan und Australien spielen.

Doch wenn Fußball schon bekannt ist, dann ist Cricket es erst recht – es ist für die ‚Trinbagoer' wie Essen, Trinken und Karneval vereint. Der rekordverdächtige Schlagmann Brian Lara ist ein Held der Republik, der seine Karriere auf einem Dorfplatz in Cantaro begann. Sport ist in Trinidad und Tobago genauso Teil des täglichen Lebens wie Musik und Feiern, ob es sich nun um eine hitzige Runde des Quartettspiels ‚All Fours' im Rumladen handelt oder um die Cricket-Weltmeisterschaft im Queen's Park Oval. Ob Sie sich also nach Action oder Entspannung sehnen, eine Mischung aus Vergangenheit und Gegenwart oder ein völlig einzigartiges karibisches Erlebnis suchen, sind Sie in Trinidad und Tobago genau richtig.

GEGENÜBERLIEGENDE SEITE
Die blaue Grotte ist in den Gasparee Höhlen, die einmal von den Piraten und von den Schmugglern benutzt wurden
Photo: Stephen Broadbridge

FACING PAGE
The Blue Grotto is located in the Gasparee Caves which were once used by pirates and smugglers
Photo: Stephen Broadbridge

Trinidad y Tobago: una experiencia única del Caribe

Situada en una región célebre por su belleza natural y su diversidad cultural, la República de Trinidad y Tobago se compone de dos islas hermanas (5.128 km²) que han conservado su especial singularidad. A diferencia de las formaciones volcánicas, de piedra caliza y coralinas del norte, estas zonas –las más sureñas de la cadena de islas de las Antillas Menores– comparten geología con la masa continental sudamericana, a la que una vez estuvieron unidas. La Cordillera Norte de Trinidad es donde realmente acaban los Andes. El pasado en común con Sudamérica explica por qué la flora y fauna de ambas islas es muy superior en diversidad y cantidad a la de cualquier otra isla caribeña.

Sin embargo, la singularidad de Trinidad y Tobago no se limita a sus recursos naturales, entre los que se encuentran *Pitch Lake* en Trinidad y la Reserva de Bosque Central de Tobago –el bosque tropical protegido más antiguo del hemisferio oeste–. Si bien mayormente de forma involuntaria, la historia ha conspirado para crear en Trinidad una de las sociedades más cosmopolitas y una de las culturas más multiétnicas del mundo. Por otro lado, en Tobago, y en la era de Internet, ha sobrevivido con orgullo una de las culturas africanas mejor afianzadas del Caribe.

Trinidad estuvo habitada originalmente por tribus amerindias de la zona noroeste de Sudamérica, quienes la llamaron "Iere" o tierra del colibrí. Su nombre actual le fue dado por Cristóbal Colón al divisar tres colinas en su costa sur en 1498. Tobago conserva el nombre amerindio del tabaco, un vestigio de una de las obsesiones europeas que, como el oro y más tarde el azúcar, dominarían la historia de las islas durante la época colonial.

Mientras holandeses, letones, franceses e ingleses se disputaban Tobago en un intento de lograr el sueño de ser "tan rico como un hacendado de Tobago", Trinidad languidecía y, hasta finales del siglo XVIII, fue un remanso de paz en el imperio colonial español. El llamamiento de la Corona de España a potenciales pobladores de fe católica romana provocó una afluencia de hacendados franceses, que llegaron con sus esclavos africanos de Martinica, Granada y Haití.

Estos fueron los comienzos de la Trinidad moderna. Los franceses talaron los bosques para hacer plantaciones, introdujeron el carnaval y el *joie de vivre* criollo que se convertiría en los cimientos de la cultura "Trini", una vez aliada con la de los esclavos. Cuando los británicos llegaron en 1797, se encontraron gobernando una colonia que hablaba francés criollo y estaba gobernada por leyes españolas. Tras la Independencia final en 1838, la cultura "Trini" se volvió incluso más colorida, con trabajadores contratados provenientes de China, India y Madeira, esclavos africanos liberados en el mar por la marina británica, vendedores ambulantes del Oriente Medio... Todos ellos se unieron en la evolución de una de las sociedades más mestizas, creativas y armónicas del planeta. Cristianos, hindúes y musulmanes conviven en estrecha proximidad y dan verdadero sentido a lo que afirman los trinitenses: "All a wee is one" ("cada poquito cuenta").

El carnaval, el calipso y las bandas de percusión típicas del Caribe son sólo algunas de las singulares expresiones de esta sociedad, logros desproporcionados comparados con su verdadero tamaño. La cultura multiétnica de Trinidad se conoce localmente como

Foto: Stephen Broadbridge

"callaloo" –el nombre de una exquisita sopa de típicos ingredientes–. Esta cultura se distingue inmediatamente por su uso creativo del idioma, por su arquitectura que va desde los "Siete Magníficos" del *Queen's Park Savannah* a los *mandir* y mezquitas existentes por todo el país, así como por su cocina que recurre a la herencia africana, india y china.

Trinidad, como su isla hermana de menor tamaño, es sin duda muy agraciada. Emplazado al sur de una zona de devastadores huracanes, este paradisíaco refugio disfruta de unos recursos energéticos –petróleo, gas natural y derivados petroquímicos– que lo han convertido en el centro financiero, comercial e industrial del Caribe del Este, además de en la indiscutible capital festera de la región. La capital del país, Puerto España, combina un pasado colonial con todas las amenidades y el estilo de vida de una metrópolis del siglo XXI. Modernos edificios emblemáticos como el complejo de la *National Library* y los rascacielos que bordean *Brian Lara Promenade* en la plaza de la Independencia, se integran con el antiguo estilo del edificio parlamentario de *Red House* y los intricados calados ornamentales de las coloridas casas de madera en los barrios residenciales. A lo largo de la costa de la península occidental, los centros comerciales *drive-in*, los condominios y los bloques de apartamentos de lujo manifiestan la voluntad de Trinidad de entregarse al futuro.

Una de las muchas paradojas de Trinidad es que, a tan sólo una corta distancia en coche de la bulliciosa capital, es posible pasear por el pasado en pueblos indios rurales, donde las banderas de rezo hindúes ondean en el aire y las carretas tiradas por bueyes y cargadas con caña de azúcar son tan fáciles de ver como los caimanes cruzando la carretera.

San Fernando, en el sur, es la segunda ciudad de Trinidad y gran parte de su importancia se debe a su proximidad a los pozos petrolíferos tanto terrestres como marinos. Chaguanas, en la llanura central, es quizá la isla de más rápido crecimiento urbano, mientras que Point Fortin es otro asentamiento de la faja petrolífera. Arima, en el este, es una antigua ciudad del cacao cuyo distrito de Santa Rosa alberga a los descendientes de los habitantes caribes originales de las islas.

De la población total de 1,3 millones de habitantes de la República, sólo hay 50.000 que viven en Tobago, la mayoría descendientes de africanos. El folclore africano y los ritmos africanos de la música del *tambrin* sobreviven en los pueblos de más altitud como Moriah y Whim y cada año se exhiben en el *Heritage Festival*. Scarborough es la única ciudad de tamaño considerable y la "Isla Tranquila" se enorgullece, y con razón, de su ritmo de vida más lento. Ir de fiesta en Trinidad y relajarse en Tobago: he aquí un buen consejo para cualquier visitante. Con sus playas prístinas y los mejores lugares para bucear en el Caribe del Este, Tobago ha desarrollado un mercado de nicho para el ecoturismo sostenible. Se trata de un tipo de turismo que contrasta con el de islas de urbanizaciones cerradas, inclusivas y con afluencias masivas.

Puede que el carnaval de Trinidad haya sido el causante de que ahora se la conozca mundialmente. Hace poco, sin embargo, Trinidad y Tobago ha honrado al mundo con su equipo de fútbol, los Soca Warriors, quienes jugaron con brío en las finales de la Copa Mundial del 2006 en Alemania. El capitán del equipo, Dwight Yorke de Tobago, y Russell Latapy de Trinidad eran ambos veteranos de la formación de 1989 y ahora se encuentran entre los primeros de un número cada vez mayor de futbolistas locales que juegan profesionalmente en Europa, América, Japón y Australia.

Y si el fútbol tiene un lugar destacado para los trinitenses, el críquet es como la comida, la bebida y el mismísimo carnaval. El plusmarquista bateador Brian Lara, un héroe en las islas hermanas, comenzó su carrera en un campo de pueblo en Cantaro. El deporte tiene tanta importancia como la música y las fiestas en el estilo de vida de Trinidad y Tobago, ya se trate de una acalorada partida *all fours* de cartas en la taberna o de la Copa Mundial de Críquet en el *Queen's Park Oval*. Si lo que busca es mucha acción y relajación total, el pasado vivo en el presente y una experiencia caribeña completamente única, todo lo va a encontrar en Trinidad y Tobago.

Trinité-et-Tobago: une expérience caribéenne unique

Dans une région renommée pour sa beauté naturelle et sa culture variée, la République de Trinité-et-Tobago, formée de deux îles (5 128 m2), se distingue par sa singularité. Contrairement aux formations volcaniques ou calcaires et coralliennes au nord, ces îles situées à l'extrême sud des Petites Antilles présentent une géologie semblable à celle du continent sud américain auquel elles étaient rattachées jadis. Les collines de *Northern Range* de Trinité sont là où se terminent réellement les Andes, et le passé sud américain des deux îles explique la richesse et l'abondance de la faune et la flore inégalées par aucune autre île des Caraïbes.

Mais la singularité de Trinité-et-Tobago ne se limite pas à ses ressources naturelles, notamment le *Pitch Lake* de Trinité et la réserve de la forêt tropicale de Tobago (la plus vieille forêt tropicale protégée dans l'hémisphère occidental). En effet, l'histoire a conspiré, largement involontairement, pour créer à Trinité l'une des sociétés les plus cosmopolites au monde ainsi qu'une des cultures les plus multiethniques ; tandis qu'à Tobago survit fièrement, à l'ère de l'Internet, l'une des plus fortes cultures africaines au sein des Caraïbes.

A l'origine colonisée par les tribus amérindiennes de la côte nord-ouest de l'Amérique du sud, qui la surnommèrent "Iere" (Pays des Colibris), Trinité doit son nom actuel à Christophe Colombe, qui aperçut trois collines surplombant la côte sud en 1498. Tobago a gardé le nom amérindien pour « tabac », souvenir d'une des obsessions européennes, qui comme celles pour l'or et le sucre, domina l'histoire des îles au cours de l'ère coloniale.

Alors que les Hollandais, les Lettons, les Français et les Anglais se disputèrent Tobago dans l'espoir de réaliser leur rêve de devenir "aussi riche qu'un planteur tobagodien", Trinité demeura un coin perdu de l'empire colonial espagnol jusqu'à la fin du XVIII siècle. L'appel de la Couronne Espagnole pour des colons catholiques engendra un afflux de planteurs français accompagnés de leurs esclaves africains provenant de Martinique, Grenade et Haïti.

Ce fut la naissance de la Trinité moderne. Les Français abattirent les forêts pour leurs plantations, introduisirent le carnaval et la joie de vivre créole, qui deviendront l'essence de la culture 'Trini' conjuguée à celle des esclaves. Lorsque les Britanniques débarquèrent en 1797, ils se retrouvèrent à la tête d'une colonie parlant le créole français gouvernée par la loi espagnole. Après l'abolition de l'esclavage en 1838, la culture « Trini » ne fit que s'enrichir: des ouvriers sous contrat importés de Chine, d'Inde et de l'île de Madère, des esclaves africains affranchis en mer par la Marine britannique, et des mercantis du Moyen-Orient vinrent tous apporter leur touche de saveur à l'évolution de l'une des sociétés les plus mixtes, créatives et harmonieuses de la planète. Ici, les chrétiens, les hindous et les musulmans vivent côte à côte, donnant un réel sens au dicton « trinbagonien » *All a wee is one* (Nous ne faisons qu'un).

Carnaval, *calypso* et *steelband* ne sont que quelques-unes des expressions uniques à cette société, exploit hors de toute proportion considérant sa taille. La culture multiethnique de Trinité, connue là-bas sous le nom de *'callaloo'* (une soupe riche composée d'ingrédients caractéristiques), transparaît instantanément dans son usage inventif de la langue, son architecture (des *'Magnificent Seven'* du *Queen's Park Savannah* aux Mandirs et mosquées érigés à travers le pays), et sa cuisine, résultat de son héritage africain, indien et chinois.

Trinité, tout comme son île jumelle plus petite, est sans aucun doute bénite. Située au sud de la ceinture des ouragans dévastateurs, ce havre de paix jouit de ressources en énergie (pétrole, gaz naturel et produits pétrochimiques associés) qui l'ont transformée en centre financier, commercial et industriel de l'Est des Caraïbes, tout comme en capitale de la fête incontestée de la région. La capitale du pays, Port d'Espagne, conjugue un passé colonial aux équipements et au style de vie d'une métropole du 21ième siècle. Les bâtiments modernes emblématiques tels que le nouveau complexe de la *National Library* et les gratte-ciels bordant la *Brian Lara Promenade* sur la place de l'Indépendance, viennent compléter le style ancien du bâtiment abritant le parlement, la *Red House*, et le découpage complexe des maisons en bois, *gingerbread houses*, de la banlieue. Le long de la côte de la péninsule occidentale, les centres commerciaux drive-in, des immeubles et bloques d'appartements de luxe témoignent de la volonté de Trinité d'embrasser l'avenir.

Mais l'un des nombreux paradoxes de Trinité est qu'à quelques kilomètres des rues animées de la capitale, on peut s'égarer dans le passé en se baladant dans les villages ruraux indiens. Il n'est pas rare d'y voir des drapeaux de prière hindous flotter au gré du vent et des charrettes tirées par des bœufs transporter des cargaisons de canne à sucre, pas plus qu'un caïman se promener le long de la route.

San Fernando, dans le sud, est la deuxième plus grande ville de Trinité et doit son importance principalement à sa proximité de champs de pétrole aussi bien terrestres que marins. Chaguanas, sur la plaine centrale, est probablement le centre urbain connaissant la plus forte expansion sur l'île, alors que Point Fortin est une autre ville située à proximité de gisements pétrolifères. A l'est, Arima est une ancienne ville productrice de cacao dont le quartier de Santa Rosa abrite les descendants des Caribes, habitants originaires de l'île.

Sur les 1,3 millions d'habitants de la République, à peine 50 000 sont tobagodiens, la plupart d'origine africaine. Le folklore et les rythmes de musique *tambrin* africains ont survécu dans des villages au sommet des collines, tels que Moriah et Whim, et sont présentés lors du *Heritage Festival* annuel. Scarborough est la seule ville d'une taille plus ou moins grande, et « l'île tranquille » est fière, à juste titre, de son style de vie bien plus paisible. Un bon conseil pour tout visiteur : fête à Trinité et détente au Tobago. Avec ses plages immaculées et les meilleurs sites de plongée dans l'Est des Caraïbes, le Tobago a développé un créneau pour l'écotourisme, contraste avec les îles offrant stations et clubs balnéaires all-inclusive et barricadés enregistrant des arrivées massives de touristes.

Même si c'est son carnaval qui lui a donné sa renommée mondiale, Trinité-et-Tobago a récemment épaté la scène internationale avec son équipe de football, les Soca Warriors, qui ont joué avec brio en finales de la Coupe du Monde 2006 en Allemagne. Le capitaine de l'équipe, le tobagodien Dwight Yorke, et le trinidadien Russell Latapy, tous deux vétérans de l'équipe de 1989, font partie des premiers joueurs du pays, dont le nombre ne cesse d'augmenter, à jouer professionnellement en Europe, USA, Japon et Australie.

Mais si le football est très en vue à Trinité-et-Tobago, le cricket lui est mis sur le même pied que la cuisine, la boisson et le carnaval. Le batteur détenteur de nombreux records, Brian Lara, est un des héros des deux îles. Il commença sa carrière sur le terrain du village de Cantaro. Dans le style de vie « tribagonien », le sport joue un rôle aussi important que la musique et la fête, qu'il s'agisse d'une partie de cartes passionnée *all fours* dans le magasin de rhum, ou de la Coupe du Monde du Cricket au *Queen's Park Oval*. Si vous recherchez à la fois action et détente, avec le passé côtoyant le présent, et une expérience caribéenne tout à fait unique, Trinité-et-Tobago est juste ce qu'il vous faut.

Trinidad e Tobago: un'esperienza caribica unica

Anche in una regione rinomata per le sue bellezze naturali e le sue diversità culturali, la repubblica delle isole gemelle di Trinidad e Tobago (5.128 kmq) è del tutto unica. A differenza delle formazioni vulcaniche o di pietra calcarea e corallina delle isole a settentrione, la geografia di questi avamposti meridionali della catena delle Piccole Antille è comune con quella della terraferma del continente sudamericano, al quale erano una volta uniti. La catena settentrionale (Northern Range) di Trinidad è la vera coda delle Ande e questa storia spiega perché la diversità e la quantità della flora e della fauna di entrambe le isole sono insuperate da qualsiasi altra isola caribica.

L'unicità di Trinidad e Tobago non è però limitata alle sue risorse naturali, che comprendono il Lago Pitch di Trinidad e la riserva forestale centrale di Tobago – la più antica foresta tropicale protetta dell'emisfero occidentale. La storia ha congiurato, in gran parte involontariamente, per creare a Trinidad una società tra le più cosmopolite e una cultura tra le più multietniche del mondo, mentre a Tobago sopravvive con fierezza nell'era di Internet una delle culture africane più solide dei Caraibi.

Popolata originariamente da tribù amerindiane provenienti dall'angolo nordoccidentale dell'America del sud, che la chiamavano «Iere» (terra del colibrì), Trinidad deve il suo nome moderno a Cristoforo Colombo, che avvistò tre colline sulla costa meridionale dell'isola nel 1498. Tobago conserva il nome amerindiano del tabacco, ricordo di una delle ossessioni europee che, come l'oro e lo zucchero, dominarono la storia delle isole durante l'epoca coloniale.

Mentre olandesi, lettoni, francesi e inglesi si disputavano l'isola di Tobago, nell'intento di realizzare il sogno di diventare «ricchi come un colono di Tobago», Trinidad rimase un angolo depresso dell'impero coloniale spagnolo fino al tardo settecento. L'appello della corona spagnola ai colonizzatori cattolici portò a una grande affluenza di coloni francesi provenienti, assieme ai loro schiavi africani, da Martinica, Grenada e Haiti.

Questo sviluppo segnò l'inizio della storia moderna di Trinidad. I francesi sgombrarono il terreno dalle foreste per creare piantagioni, portarono il carnevale e la *joie de vivre* dei creoli che, assieme alla cultura degli schiavi, diventarono gli elementi fondamentali della cultura *Trini*. Quando arrivarono i britannici, nel 1797, si trovarono a regnare su una colonia di gente di lingua creola francese ma governata da leggi spagnole. Dopo l'emancipazione completa del 1838, la miscela di spezie diventò ancora più saporita: lavoratori a contratto importati dalla Cina, dall'India e da Madeira, schiavi africani liberati in mare dalla marina britannica e mercanti dal Medio Oriente si unirono all'evoluzione di una delle società più miste, creative e armoniose del pianeta. Cristiani, induisti e musulmani vivono fianco a fianco, dando un vero significato al detto dei *Trinbagonians* (gli abitanti di Trinidad e Tobago) «All a wee is one», per dire che sono un popolo completamente unito.

Il carnevale, la musica calypso e i tamburi d'acciaio sono solo uno dei modi di espressione unici di questa società: delle realizzazioni del tutto sproporzionate alle sue effettive dimensioni. Definita nelle isole con il termine *callaloo* (una ricca minestra di ingredienti ben distinti), la cultura multietnica di Trinidad è immediatamente evidente dall'uso fantasioso della lingua, dall'architettura (dai "Magnifici Sette" del Queen's Park Savannah ai mandir e alle moschee sparse per tutto il paese), e dalla cucina, ispirata alle sue origini africane, indiane e cinesi.

Come Tobago, sua sorella minore, Trinidad è indubbiamente beata. Situata a sud della devastante fascia degli uragani, questo rifugio sicuro ha le proprie risorse energetiche (petrolio, gas naturale e prodotti petrolchimici associati) che l'hanno trasformata in centro finanziario, commerciale e industriale dei Caraibi orientali, nonché incontrastata capitale del divertimento di tutta la regione. La capitale del paese, Port of Spain, unisce al suo passato coloniale tutte le strutture e lo stile di vita di una metropoli del ventunesimo secolo. Edifici moderni come il nuovo complesso della biblioteca nazionale e i grattacieli che fiancheggiano la Brian Lara Promenade di Independence Square fanno da complemento allo stile antico della Red House (l'edificio del parlamento) e le decorazioni traforate delle case di legno dei sobborghi, chiamate *gingerbread houses* o case di zenzero. Lungo la costa della penisola occidentale, centri commerciali, condomini e appartamenti di lusso sono tutti dimostrazioni della volontà di Trinidad di abbracciare il futuro.

Ma uno degli aspetti più paradossali di Trinidad è che a pochi chilometri dal trambusto della capitale si può fare un salto indietro nella storia, ritrovandosi in uno dei villaggi indiani, dove svolazzano nel vento le bandierine di preghiera induiste e dove un carro trainato da buoi e carico di canne da zucchero è comune quanto un caimano che percorre la strada con andatura ondulante.

San Fernando, a sud, è la seconda città di Trinidad e deve molta della sua importanza alla vicinanza delle zone petrolifere, sia terrestri che marittime. Chaguanas, sulla pianura centrale, è probabilmente il centro urbano che sta crescendo più rapidamente, mentre Point Fortin è un altro insediamento della fascia petrolifera e Arima, a est, è un antico centro di produzione del cacao, il cui distretto di Santa Rosa è luogo di origine dei discendenti dei primi abitanti caribici dell'isola.

Solo 50.000 degli 1,3 milioni di abitanti della repubblica sono originari di Tobago e principalmente di discendenza africana. Il folklore africano e il ritmo della musica dei tamburini sopravvivono ancora nei villaggi collinari di Moriah e Whim, e vengono esibiti ogni anno durante il Heritage Festival. Scarborough è l'unico centro che abbia le dimensioni di una vera città e la *Tranquil Isle* o isola tranquilla, come viene chiamata, è giustamente fiera del suo stile di vita molto più calmo. Fai festa a Trinidad e riposati a Tobago è un buon consiglio per qualsiasi visitatore. Con le sue spiagge incontaminate e dei centri di esplorazione subacquea tra i migliori dei Caraibi orientali, Tobago ha sviluppato un mercato di nicchia per l'ecoturismo sostenibile, a differenza di altre isole con centri turistici recintati, grandi affluenze di turisti e vacanze tutto compreso.

Sebbene sia il carnevale ad aver reso famosa Trinidad in tutto il mondo, Trinidad e Tobago ha recentemente onorato la scena mondiale con la sua squadra di calcio, i *Soca Warriors*, che hanno dato uno spettacolo di grande energia alle finali della Coppa del Mondo 2006 in Germania. Il capitano della squadra, Dwight Yorke, nativo di Tobago, e Russel Latapy, di Trinidad, erano entrambi veterani della squadra del 1989 e sono tra i primi di un crescente numero di calciatori che ormai giocano da professionisti in Europa, America, Giappone e Australia.

Ma benché il calcio sia uno sport di alto profilo, è il cricket a fare da cibo, bibita e carnevale di tutti i *Trinbagonians*. Il battitore da primato Brian Lara è un eroe di entrambe le isole che iniziò la sua carriera sul campo da cricket del paesino di Cantaro. Che si tratti di una partita di briscola in una *rum shop* (bottega del rum) o di una partita dei mondiali di cricket al Queen's Park Oval, nello stile di vita di Trinidad e Tobago lo sport è importante quanto la musica e la voglia di far festa. Cercate una vacanza superdinamica ma anche un posto per rilassarvi in tranquillità? Un'esperienza caribica totalmente unica in un luogo dove il passato è intrecciato con il presente? Troverete tutto questo a Trinidad e Tobago.

TRINIDAD AND TOBAGO OVERSEAS MISSIONS

BELGIUM
Embassy of the Republic of
Trinidad and Tobago
Avenue de La Faisanderie 14
1150 Brussels
Tel: 011-322 762 9400
Fax: 011-322772 2783
Email: info@embtrinbago.be

BRAZIL
Embassy of the Republic of
Trinidad and Tobago
SHIS QL 02 Conjunto 02, Casa 01
71665-028 Brasilia DF
Tel: 011-5561 3365 3466
Fax: 011 5561 3365 1733
Email: trinbago@terra.com.br
Telex: 611844 EBTTBR

CANADA
High Commission of the Republic
of Trinidad and Tobago
Third Level, 200 First Avenue
Ottawa, Ontario K1S 2G6
Tel: 1-613 232 2418/9
Fax: 1-613 232 4349
Email: Ottawa@ttmissions.com
Web: www.ttmissions.com

Consulate General of the
Republic of Trinidad and Tobago
2005 Sheppard Avenue East
Suite 303
Toronto, Ontario M2J 5B4
Tel: 1-416 495 9442
Fax: 1-416 495 6934
E: congen@ttconsulaetoronto.com
Web: www.ttconsulatetoronto.com

INDIA
High Commission of the Republic
of Trinidad and Tobago
6/25 Shanti Niketan
New Delhi, 110021
Tel: 011-911 1 2411 8427
Fax: 011-911 1 2411 8463
Email: hcreptt25@vsn.com

JAMAICA
High Commission of the Republic
of Trinidad and Tobago
First Life Building, 3rd Floor
60 Knutsford Boulevard
Kingston 5
Tel: 1-876 926 5739
Fax: 1-876 926 5801
Email: t&thckgn@infochan.com

LONDON
High Commission of the Republic
of Trinidad and Tobago
42 Belgrave Square
London SW1X 8NT
Tel: 01-144 207 245 9351
Fax: 01-144 207 823 1065
Email: tthc@btconnect.com

NIGERIA
High Commission of the Republic
of Trinidad and Tobago
7 Casablanca Street, Wuse II, Abuja
Tel: 011-234 9 523 7534
Fax: 011-234 9 523 7684
E: trinitobagoabj@yahoo.co.uk

SOUTH AFRICA
High Commission of the Republic
of Trinidad and Tobago
258 Lawley Street, Waterkloof
Pretoria
Tel: 011-271 2460 9688
Fax: 011-271 2346 7302
Email: tthcpretoria@telkomsa.net

UNITED NATIONS
Permanent Mission of Trinidad
and Tobago to the United Nations
37-39 rue de Vermont
1202 Geneva, Switzerland
Tel: 011-4122 918 0380
Fax: 011-4122 734 9138
E: Mission.Trinidad-Tobago@ties.itu.int

Permanent Mission of Trinidad
and Tobago to the United Nations
820 Second Avenue, 5th Floor
New York NY 10017
Tel: 1-212 697 7620
Fax: 1-212 682 3580
Email: tto@UN.INT

UNITED STATES OF AMERICA
Consulate General of the
Republic of Trinidad and Tobago
1000 Brickell Avenue, Suite 800
Miami Fl. 33131-3047
Tel: 1-305 374 2199
Fax: 1-305 374 3199
Email: ttmiami@worldnet.att.net

Consulate General of the
Republic of Trinidad and Tobago
475 Fifth Avenue, 4th Floor
New York NY 10017
Tel: 1-212 682 7272
Fax: 1-212 986 2146
Email: consulate@ttcgny.com

Embassy of the Republic of
Trinidad and Tobago
1708 Massachusetts Avenue NW
Washington DC 20036-1975
Tel: 1-202 467 6490
Fax: 1-202 785 3130
Email: info@ttembwash.com

VENEZUELA
Embassy of the Republic of
Trinidad and Tobago
Quinta Serrana, 4ta Avenida,
Entre 7a Y 8A Transversales,
Altamira, Apartado de Este 61322
Caracas 1060A
Tel: 011-58 212 261 3748
Fax: 011-58 212 261 9801
Email: embassytt@cantv.net

INTERNATIONAL DIALLING CODE: 868

ACCOMMODATION

Abercromby Inn
101 Abercromby Street
Tel: 624 3858

Acajou Hotel, Restaurant & Bar
209 Paria Main Road, Toco
Tel: 670 3771
Email: info@AcajouTrinidad.com

Airport View Guest House
St Helena Vlg, Piarco
Tel: 669 4186

Alicia's House
7 Coblentz Gardens, St Anns
Tel: 623 2802
Email: info@aliciashouse.com

Alicia's Palace
1 3/4MM Lady Chancellor Hill, St
Anns, Port of Spain
Tel: 624 8553

Ambassador Hotel
99A Long Cir Road, St James
Tel: 628 9000

Arnos Vale Hotel
Franklyn Road, Arnos Vale Estate
Tobago
Tel: 639 2881
E: reservations@arnosvalehotel.com

Arthur's By The Sea
Crown Point, Tobago
Tel: 639 0196

Bacolet Bay Apartment Hotel
Bacolet Street, Scarborough
Tobago
Tel: 639 2955

Baja Del Sol Bed & Breakfast
23 Fifth Street, E Trincity
Tel: 760 1328

Bayview Beach Resort & Marina
Gaspar Grande Island
Chaguaramas
Tel: 627 9728

Bel Air International Airport Hotel
Piarco Airport, Piarco
Tel: 669 4771

Belleviste Apartments
Sandy Point, Tobago
Tel: 639 9351
Email: bellevis@tstt.net.tt

Blanchisseuse Laguna Mar Beach
Hotel
65 1/2 Paria Main Road
Tel: 669 2963

Blue Haven Hotel
Bacolet Bay, Tobago
Tel: 660 7500
E: reservations@bluehavenhotel.com

Blue Horizon Resort Co Ltd
Jacamar Drive, Mt Irvine, Tobago
Tel: 639 0432
E: sales@blue-horizonresort.com

Blue Waters Inn
Batteau Bay, Speyside, Tobago
Tel: 660 4341
Email: bwi@bluewatersinn.com
Web: www.bluewatersinn.com

Brandsville
88-90 Pike Street
Section 'M' Campbelville
Georgetown
GUYANA
Tel: 226 1133, 226 6162
Fax: 231 7001
Email: brandsville@gol.net.gy

Campus Villas
Mahamdoo Terrace, St Augustine
Tel: 663 6902

Cara Suites
Southern Main Road, Claxton Bay
Tel: 659 2271
E: carasuitespap@carahotels.com
Web: www.carahotels.com

Carnetta's Inn Ltd
99 Saddle Road, Maraval
Tel: 628 2732

Castlewhite Hotel & Holiday Resort
Studley Park, Tobago
Tel: 660 2905

Cedar Ridge Towers
56 Third Street, Maraval
Tel: 628 6526

Chaconia Hotel
106 Saddle Road, Maraval
Tel: 628 0941

Chaguaramas Hotel & Convention
Centre
Western Main Road, Chaguaramas
Tel: 634 2379

Cinnamon Court
148 Clifton Hill
Tel: 648 0752

Coblentz Inn Boutique Hotel
44 Coblentz Avenue, Cascade
Tel: 621 0541
Email: coblentzinn@tstt.net.tt

Coconut Cove Holiday Beach Club
33-36 Calypson Road, Manzanilla
Tel: 691 5939
Email: cove2b@yahoo.com

Coco Reef Resort
P O Box 434, Tobago
Tel: 639 8571
Email: cocoreef-
tobago@trinidad.net

Cocrico Inn
Plymouth, Tobago
Tel: 639 2961

Conrado Beach Resort Hotel Ltd
Pigeon Point, Tobago
Tel: 639 0145

Coral Cove Marina
Western Main Road, Chaguaramas
Tel: 634 2040

Courtyard By Marriott
Invaders Bay, Audrey Jeffers
Highway, Port of Spain
Tel: 627 5555

Crews Inn Hotel & Yachting Centre
P O Box 518, Chaguaramas Bay
Tel: 634 4384
Email: crewsinn@tstt.net.tt

Crooks Apartments
Stores Bay Local Road, Tobago
Tel: 639 8492

Crowne Plaza
P O Box 1017, Wrightson Road
Port of Spain
Tel: 625 3361
Email: eoffice@crowneplaza.co.tt

Crown Point Beach Hotel Ltd
PO Box 223, Scarborough, Tobago
Tel: 639 8781
Fax: 639 8731
E: crownpoint@sunsurfsand.com

Crusoe's Holiday Apartments
33 Store Bay, Tobago
Tel: 639 7789

Crystal Stream Hotel & Bar
Golden Grove Road, Arouca
Tel: 642 4310

Cuffie River Nature Retreat
Runnemede, Tobago
Tel: 678 9020

Douglas Apartments & Car Rentals
Crown Point, Tobago
Tel: 639 7723

Enchanted Waters Hotel
Shirvan Road, Buccoo, Tobago
Tel: 639 9481
Email: info@kpresorts.com

Errol Lau Hotel
66-68 Edward Street
Port of Spain
Tel: 625 4381

Esterel Hotel
Cumana, Toco
Tel: 670 4772
Email: stay@hotelesterel.com

Fabiennes Guest House
15 Belle Smythe Street, Woodbrook
Tel: 622 2773

Footprints Eco Resorts
Culloden Bay Road, Tobago
Tel: 660 0416
Email: footprints@trinidad.net

Forty Winks Inn
24 Warner Street, Newtown
Tel: 622 0484
Email: pam@fortywinksst.com

Golden Thistle Hotel
Store Bay Road
Crown Point
Tobago
Tel: 639 8521
Email: goldenthistle@tstt.net.tt

Golf View Apartments Ltd
Old Grange, Mt Irvine, Tobago
Tel: 639 0979

Grafton Beach Resort
Stonehaven Bay
Black Rock
Tobago
Tel: 639 0191
Email: grafton@singhs.com

Grandville Beach Resort
Grandville Beach Road
Cedros
Tel: 690 0224

Grange Inn
Buccoo & Mt Irvine Junction
Tobago
Tel: 639 9395

Green Oak Tower Hotel
267 Santa Cruz Old Road
San Juan
Tel: 675 1593

Halyconia Inn
7 First Avenue
Cascade
Tel: 623 0008
Email: lmorris@wow.net
Web: www.halyconiainn.com

Half Moon Blue Hotel
At the donkey cart house
Bacolet Bay
Tobago
Tel: 639 3551
Email:
holidays@halfmoonblue.com
Web: www.halfmoonblue.com

Harbour View Guest House
Milford Road
Scarborough
Tel: 639 6404

Harry's Guest House
Baywatch Blvd
Mayaro
Tel: 769 6310
Web: www.harrys4u.net

Havanna Recreation Club & Hotel
California
19A Nelson Street
Arima
Tel: 667 2209

Hew Tours Hotel Reservations
Buccoo
Tobago
Tel: 639 9058

Hillcrest Haven
74 Hillcrest Avenue
Cascade
Tel: 624 1344

Hilton Tobago Golf and Spa
Resort
Tobago Plantations Estate
Lowlands
Tobago
Tel: 660 8500
Email: 660 8503
Web: www.hiltoncaribbean.com/
tobago

Hilton Trinidad & Conference
Centre
Lady Young Road
Port of Spain
Tel: 624 3211
Email:
reservations.Trinidad@hilton.com
Web: www.hiltoncaribbean.com/
trinidad

Hosanna Hotel
Santa Margarita Circular Road
St Augustine
Tel: 662 5449
Email: rest@hosannahotel.com
Web: www.hosannahoel.com

In the spirit of CSME and a unified Caribbean, we are taking the unusual step of introducing our Trinidadian friends to a beautiful Guyanese property. Welcome to Brandsville, a hotel and apartment complex situated in the heart of Georgetown. Started in 1977 as an apartment facility, the company has expanded over the years to accommodate guests with varying needs and budgets. With bed and breakfast and self-contained units and apartments, Brandsville offers a comprehensive range of services inclusive of Internet, fax and long distance connections. Our breakfast and lunch menus are a mix of Guyanese, Caribbean and Continental fare. This is the appeal of Brandsville, and once you've come here to stay you will always want to come again.

Hotel Carries On The Bay
Eastern Main Road
Manzanilla
Tel: 668 5711

Hotel Coconut Inn Ltd
Store Bay Local Road
Crown Point, Tobago
Tel: 639 8493
Email: hciltobago@yahoo.com

Hotel Tokyo
43-45 St James Street
San Fernando
Tel: 652 3257

Indigo Tobago
Horseshoe Ridge
Tobago
Tel: 639 9635

Inn On The Bay
Little Rockley Bay
Lambeau
Tobago
Tel: 639 4347

James Holiday Resort, Car
Rentals & Tours
Store Bay Beach Road
Crown Point
Tobago
Tel: 639 8929

Jimmy's Holiday Resort
Milford Road
P O Box 109
Crown Point
Tobago
Tel: 639 8292
Email: jimmys@tstt.net.tt

Johnson's Bed & Breakfast
16 Buller Street
Woodbrook
Tel: 628 7553

Johnston Apartments
Store Bay
Tobago
Tel: 639 8915
Email: johnapt@tstt.net.tt

Kapok Hotel
16-18 Cotton Hill
St Clair
Tel: 622 5765
Email: stay@kapokhotel.com

Kariwak Village (Hotel)
Store Bay Local Road
Crown Point
Tobago
Tel: 639 8442

La Calypso Tourist
Accommodation
46 French Street, Woodbrook
Tel: 622 4077

Las Cuevas Beach Lodge
North Coast Road
Las Cuevas
Tel: 669 6945

Le Chateau Hotel & Bar
19 Buen Intento Road, P/Town
Tel: 655 0559

Le Grande Almandier Guest House
2 Hosang Street
Grande Rivere
Tel: 670 1013
E: info@legrandealmandier.com

Le Grand Courlan Spa resort
Stonehaven Bay
Black Rock
Tobago
Tel: 639 9667
Email: legrand@singhs.com
W: www.legrandcourlan-resort.com

Le Sportel Inn
Macoya Road
Tunapuna
TelL 663 3905

Manta Lodge
Speyside
Tobago
Tel: 660 5268

Maracas Bay Hotel Ltd
Maracas Bay
Maracas
Tel: 669 1914

Melbourne Inn
7 French Street
Woodbrook
Tel: 623 4006

Mikanne Hotel Ltd
15 Railway Avenue
P A Pierre
Tel: 659 2584

Monique's Guest House
114-116 Saddle Road
Maraval
Tel: 628 3334

Motown Guest House
64 Picton Street
Newtown
Tel: 628 3828

Mount Irvine Bay Hotel & Golf
Club
Mt Irvine
Tobago
Tel: 639 8872

Mount Marie Guest House
Mount Marie
Scarborough
Tobago
Tel: 639 2104

Normandie
10 Nook Avenue
St Anns
Port of Spain
Tel: 624 1181
Email: home@normandiett.com

Ocean Point Holiday Resort
Milford Road
Lowlands
Tobago
Tel: 639 0973

Par-May-La's Inn
53 Picton Street
Newtown
Tel: 628 2008
Email: parmaylas@trinidad.net

Paria Suites
South Trunk Road
La Romain
Tel: 697 2742
Email: info@pariasuites.com

Pax Guest House & Tea Garden
Tunapuna
Tel: 662 4048

Piarco International Hotel
8-10 Golden Grove Road
Piarco
Tel: 669 3030

Picton Court Apartments
109 Woodford Street
Newtown
Port of Spain
Tel: 637 9770

Plantation Beach Villas
Stonehaven Bay
Black Rock, Tobago
Tel: 639 9377
Email: plantationbeach@tstt.net.tt

Palm Tree Village
Little Rockley Bay
Tobago
Tel: 639 4347

Rainbow Resort
Crown Point
Tobago
Tel: 639 9940

Ramona Beach House
Gill Road, Mayaro
Tel: 630 4135

Royal Hotel
46-54 Royal Road, San Fernando
Tel: 652 4881
Email: info@royalhoteltt.com

Royal Palm Suite Hotel
7 Saddle Road, Maraval
Tel: 628 5086
Email: royalpalm@trinidad.net

Rovanel's
Resort & Conference Centre
Store Bay Local Road
Crown Point, Tobago
Tel: 639 9666

Salybia Nature Resort & Spa
Trinidad
Salybia Village
Tel: 691 3210

Sanctuary Villa Resort
Grafton Estate, Tobago
Tel: 639 9556
Email: info@sanctuaryvillas.com

Sandy Point Beach Club
Crown Point, Tobago
Tel: 639 0820
Email: sandypoint@tstt.net.tt

Seahorse Inn
Stonehaven Bay
Grafton Beach
Tobago
Tel: 639 0686
Email: seahorse@trinidad.net

Seaville Chateau
Belle Air Road
Tel: 660 6146

Serenity Inn
La Pastora Road
Santa Cruz
Tel: 676 2674
Email: serenityinn@tstt.net.tt

Sherwood Park Apartments
Sherwood Park
Tobago
Tel: 639 7151

South Western Court
16 Guapo Road
Pt Fortin
Tel: 648 0075

Speyside Inn
Windward Road
Speyside, Tobago
Tel: 660 4852

Stonehaven Villas
Grafton Estate, Tobago
Tel: 639 0361

Store Bay Holiday Resort
Store Bay Local Road
Crown Point, Tobago
Tel: 639 8810

Success Inn Guest House
4 Sarah Street, Laventille
Tel: 623 5504

Sundeck Suites
42-44 Picton Street, Port of Spain
Tel: 622 9560

Sunshine Holiday Apartments
Milford Road
Tobago
Tel: 639 7495

Surf Side Hotel
Tel: 639 9702 (weekdays)
Tel: 639 0614 (nights &
weekends)
Email:
hotelreservation@surfsidetobago.com
Web: www.surfsidetobago.com

Surf's Country Inn
North Coast Road
Blanch
Tel: 669 2475

Swambers Inn Restaurant & Bar
Southern Main Road
Enterprise
Tel: 672 5720

Tara's Beach House
Milford Road
Lambeau
Tobago
Tel: 639 1556

The Caribbean Lodge
32 St Augustine Circular Road
St Augustine
Tel: 645 7000

The Cascadia Hotel & Conference
Centre
Ariapita Road
St Anns
Port of Spain
Tel: 623 4208
Email:
marketing@cascadiahotel.com
Web: www.cascadiahotel.com

The Chancellor Hotel &
Conference Centre
5 St Anns Avenue
St Anns
Port of Spain
Tel: 623 0883
Web: www.thechancellor.com

The Copper Kettle Hotel &
Restaurant
66 Edward Street
Port of Spain
Tel: 625 4381

The Emerald Apartments & Plaza
11 Eastern Main Road
St Augustine
Tel: 663 8087
Email:
emeraldapartments@tstt.net.tt

The Five Star Guest House
7 French Street
Port of Spain
Tel: 623 4006

The Humming Bird Hotel
12B Store Bay Local Road
Bon Accord
Tobago
Tel: 635 0241

The Normandie Hotel &
Restaurant
10 Nook Avenue
St Anns
Port of Spain
Tel: 625 8732

The Palms Villa Resort
Signal Hill Old Road
Signal Hill
Tobago
Tel: 635 1010
Email: info@thepalmstobago.com

The Villa Maria Inn
48A Perseverance Road
Maraval
Tel: 629 8023

The Villas at Stonehaven
Black Rock
Tobago
Tel: 639 0361
Email: stonehav@tstt.net.tt
Web: www.stonehavenvillas.com

Tobago Island Suites
Corner Buccoo & Shirvan Roads
Mt Irvine
Tobago
Tel: 639 0979
Email: friends@tobagosuites.com
Web: www.tobagosuites.com

Tobago On-Line Reservation
Burnett Street
Scarborough
Tel: 639 3393

Tobago Plantations Beach & Golf
Resort
Tel: 639 8000

Tobago Villas Agency
P O Box 301, Tobago
Tel: 639 8737

Toucan Inn & Bonkers
Crown Point, Tobago
Tel: 639 7173

Trade Winds Hotel & Members Club
38 London Street, San Fernando
Tel: 652 9463
Email: delia@tradewindshotel.net

Trinidad Tourist Accommodation
37 Ariapita Avenue
Tel: 627 7114

Tropikist Beach Hotel & Resort Ltd
Crown Point, Tobago
Tel: 639 8512

Turtle Beach Hotel
Courland Bay, Plymouth
Tobago
Tel: 639 2636

Unique Hotel & Hideaway Bar
3 Dam Road
Longdenville
Tel: 672 3315

Valsayn Villa Guest House
34 Gilwell Road
Valsayn
Tel: 645 1193

Villas of Tobago Ltd
Main Road, Bon Accord
Tobago
Tel: 639 9600

Viola's Place
Lowlands
Tobago
Tel: 639 9441

V I P Holiday Resorts
Stores Bay Local Road
Crown Point, Tobago
Tel: 639 9096

Westpoint Hotel
125 Western Main Road
Chaguaramas
Tel: 634 2426

ADVERTISING

Ross Advertising Image
Consultancy &
Events Management
16 Gray Street, St Clair
Port of Spain
Tel: 622 1967/622 4306/628 0450
Fax: 622 1779
Email: ross@rossadvertising.co.tt

BOOKSELLERS

Charrans Bookstores
53 Eastern Main Road
Tunapuna
Tel: 663 1884/ 645 3878
Fax: 645 8315
E: hennycharran@hotmail.com

Ishmael Khan
20 Henry Street
Port of Spain
Tel: 623 4523
Fax: 625 7996
Email: imkhanpos@tstt.net.tt

Keith Khan's Books Etc, Ltd
58 Frederick Street
Port of Spain
Tel: 623 1201
Email: kkhan@tstt.net.tt

Lexicon Trinidad Ltd
LP#48 Boundary Road
San Juan
Tel: 675 3389
Fax: 675 3395
Email: lexicon@tstt.net.tt

Metropolitan Book Suppliers Ltd
Capital Plaza
11-13 Frederick Street
Port of Spain
Tel/Fax: 623 3462
Fax: 627 0856
E: metrobooksuppliers@tstt.net.tt

R.I.K. Services Limited
(Trinidad Book World)
104 High Street, San Fernando
Tel: 652 4824
Fax: 657 6793
Email: rik@carib-link.net
& 7 Queen Street
Port of Spain
Tel: 623 4316

BUSINESS & INDUSTRY

BP Trinidad and Tobago
5-5a Queen's Park West
Port of Spain
Tel: 623 2862
Fax: 627 7863

eTeck
The Atrium, Don Miguel Road
Extension, El Socorro
Tel: 675 1989
Email: info@eteck.co.tt

National Gas Company of
Trinidad and Tobago Ltd
Orinoco Drive
Point Lisas Industrial Estate
Box 1127 Port of Spain
Tel: 636 4662/4680
Fax: 679 2384
Email: info@ngc.co.tt

Neal & Massy Group
63 Park Street, Port of Spain
Tel: 625 3426
Fax: 627 9061
Email: nmh@neal-and-massy.com

SUEZ LNG (Trinidad and Tobago) Ltd
1st Floor, Chamber of Commerce
Building – Columbus Circle
Westmoorings
Tel: 633 1919
Fax: 633 2020

HEALTH & FITNESS

Cox & Sons Barbell Gym Health &
Fitness Centre
Milford Road, Canaan
Tel: 639 9638

E & F Health Foods
Carrington Street, Tobago
Tel: 639 3992

Randy's Back to Eden All Natural
Store
Burnett Street, Scarborough
Tel: 660 7070

Innercare Centre (Health Food
Products)
Unit 10 Crooks River Mall
Scarborough
Tel: 635 0066

Seasons
28 St James Street
San Fernando
Tel: 652 8810

Natural Balance
The Natural Medicine Centre
25 Alexandra Street
St Clair
Tel: 628 5649

NATURE PARKS

Asa Wright Nature Centre
7 3/4 Ml Blanchisseuse Road
Tel: 667 4655

REAL ESTATE

Kanhai Real Estate
242 North Stars Avenue
Malabar, Phase 2
Arima
Tel/Fax: 642 7375

RESTAURANTS

Café Coco
First Left off Pigeon Point Road
Crown Point, Tobago
Tel: 639 0996
E: cocoreef-tobago@trinidad.net

Ciao Café
Burnett Street, Scarborough
Tobago
Tel: 639 3001
Email: ciaocafe_Tobago@yahoo.it

Kariwak Village Hotel
Store Bay Road
Tobago
Tel: 639 8442
Email: kariwak@tstt.net.tt

La Terrazza
Tobago Plantations Golf Club
Lowlands
Tobago
Tel: 639 8242
Email: la.terrazzo@hotmail.com

Me Shell's Restaurant
Cnr. Shirvan Road & Old Buccoo
Road, Tobago
Tel: 631 0353
Email: meshl@tstt.net.tt

Pelican Reef Bar & Grill
Crown Point
Tobago
Tel: 660 8000

Seahorse Inn
Black Rock
Tobago
Tel: 639 0686
Web:
www.seahorseinntobago.com

Shirvan Watermill Restaurant
Shirvan Road
Mt Pleasant
Tobago
Tel: 639 0000
Email: swmill@tstt.net.tt

Shore Things
Old Milford Road
Lambeau
Tobago
Tel: 635 1072
Web: www.tobagotoday.com/
shorethings

Shutters on the Bay
Bacolet Bay
Tobago
Tel: 660 7500
Web: www.bluehavenhotel.com

The Chart House
Crown Point Beach Hotel
Crown Point
Tobago
Tel: 639 8781

The Pavilion Restaurant
The Villas at Stonehaven
Black Road
Tobago
Tel: 639 0361
Web: www.stonehavenvillas.com

ROTI SHOPS

Amin's Restaurant & Caterers
~ 243 Southern Main Road
Marabella
Tel: 658 1691
~ Southern Main Road
Couva
Tel: 636 7673
~ Cipero Street
San Fernando
Tel: 652 5108
~ Chaguanas
Tel: 672 3815
~ Princess Town
Tel: 655 1309

De Balo's Roti Shop
53 Park Street
Port of Spain
Tel: 624 7684
78 Charlotte Street
Port of Spain
Tel: 623 2256

Don's II Roti Shop
Richplain & Diego Martin Main
Rds
Tel: 633 2588

Don's Roti Shop
Crystal Stream Ave & Morne Coco
Rd
P/Valley
Tel: 637 8310

Hott Roti Shoppe
121 Coffee Street
San Fernando
Tel: 652 9465

Hott Shoppe
52 Maraval Road
Tel: 622 2858

Karamath's Roti Shop
57 Coffee Street
San Fernando
Tel: 653 1142

Khan's Roti & Tea Shop
5 Mainfield Road
Pt Fortin
Tel: 648 3423

MSM Homestyle Cooking
176 Southern Main Road
Tel: 659 0044

Patraj Roti Shop
Back Chain Street
El Socorro
Tel: 638 2479
Tragarete Road
St James
Tel: 622 6219

Roti Express
Maritime Bldg
Barataria
Tel: 638 7822

Roti Supreme
80 Queen Street
Port of Spain
Tel: 625 0846

Savoy's Roti Shop
82 Coffee Street
San Fernando
Tel: 657 0011

RUM DISTILLERS

Rum Distillers of Trinidad &
Tobago Ltd
Old Southern Main Road
Caroni
Tel: 663 1781

Trinidad Distillers Ltd
Eastern Main Road & Angostura
Streets, Laventille
Tel: 623 2501

RUM DISTRIBUTORS

Angostura Limited
The House of Angostura, Eastern
Main Road & Trinity Ave, Laventille
Tel: 623 1841

Fernandes Distillers (1973) Ltd
Eastern Main Road & Angostura
Streets, Laventille
Tel: 623 2101

Rum Distillers of Trinidad &
Tobago Ltd
Old Southern Main Road
Caroni
Tel: 663 1781

SHOPPING &
ENTERTAINMENT

Courts (Trinidad) Ltd
Megastore Complex
Churchill Roosevelt Highway
San Juan
Tel: 674 5409
Fax: 674 6667

The Falls at Westmall
Western Main Road
Westmoorings
Tel: 632 1239
Fax: 633 1245

MovieTowne Mall & Cineplex
Multicinemas Trinidad Limited
Lot D, MovieTowne Boulevard
Audrey Jeffers Highway
Port of Spain
Tel: 627 8277
Fax: 625 9552
Email: info@movietowne.com

SPORT

CWC World Cup (2007) T & T Ltd
5th Floor, Tatil Building
11 Maraval Road
Port of Spain
Tel: 628 9314
Fax: 622 5424
Email: info.trinidadandtobago
@cricketworldcup.com

TOURISM

Tourism Development Company Limited
Level 1, Maritime Centre,
#29 Tenth AVENUE, Barataria
Trinidad, West Indies
Tel: (868) 675-7034
Fax: (868) 638-7962

& Piarco International Airport
Tel: (868) 669-5196 or (868) 669-6044
Fax: (868) 669-6045
Email: tourism-info@tdc.co.tt

TOURS

A Willoughby's Tours
25-31 High Street
San Fernando
Tel: 652 7747

A J M Tours Ltd
90 Queen Street
Port of Spain
Tel: 625 3732

Alston's Travel
67 Independence Square
Port of Spain
Tel: 625 2201

Aziza Tours & Travel Services Ltd
Couva Shopping Complex
Couva
Tel: 636 5581

Blue Emperor Tours
Springflow Road
D/Martin
Tel: 637 4246

Caribbean Discovery Tours Ltd
9B Fondes Amandes Road
St Anne's
Port of Spain
Tel: 624 7281
Cell: 620 1989
Fax: 624 8596
Email: caribdis@wow.net

C M S Travel & Tours Ltd
Plaza Imperial Bldg
San Fernando
Tel: 653 0222

Carvalho's Agencies
The American Stores Building
St James
Tel: 628 1051

Chaguaramas Tours
Airway Road
Chaguaramas
Tel: 634 4227
Email: chagdev@tstt.net.tt
Web: www.chagdev.com

Corporate Tavel & Tours Ltd
1 De Verteuil Street
Woodbrook
Tel: 624 0800

E T Tours & Travel Ltd
18-21 Ramjattan Tr
Penal
Tel: 647 2504

Eniath's Travel & Tours Ltd
6 Gaston Street
Chaguanas
Tel: 672 7964

Francis Travel & Tours Services
Francis Plaza
Chaguanas
Tel: 671 5920

Hews Glass Bottom Boat Tours
Buccoo Tobago
Tel: 639 9058
Web: www.hews-tours.com

IN Joy Tours
Tel: 633 4733
Cell: 753 2775
Fax: 633 1771
Email: injoytours@hotmail.com

J C Tours & Travel Ltd
Charlotte Street & Independence Square
Port of Spain
Tel: 625 6930

Kalloo's Auto Rentals, Taxi Service & Tours
31 French Street
Port of Spain
Tel: 622 9073

Kenny's Rentals
6 Bournes Road
St James
Tel: 628 7129

Latin Tours
Valpark Shopping Plaza
Valsayn
Tel: 662 1847

Mid Eastern Travel Service
30 Southern Main Road
Curepe
Tel: 662 2437

Mississauga Travel Ltd
Triangle Mall
Penal
Tel: 647 7680

Naipaul's Tours & Travel Service Ltd
Port Authority Admin Bldg
Port of Spain
Tel: 623 5516

Nanan's Bird Sanctuary Tours
Bamboo Grove Settlement No. 1
Valsayn
Tel: 645 1305

Public Transport Service Corporation
Port of Spain
Tel: 623 2262
Tobago – Tel: 639 2293
San Fernando – Tel: 652 3705

Royale Tours & Travel Services Ltd
103D St Vincent Street, Port of Spain
Tel: 624 5603

T J's Island Cruises
South Trunk Road
Tel: 653 0408

The Travel Centre Ltd
16 Damian Street, Woodbrook
Tel: 622 0112

Transport Solutions Ltd
Piarco International Airport
Tel: 800 3131

Trinidad and Tobago Sightseeing Tours
12 Western Main Road, St James
Port of Spain
Tel: 628 1051
Fax: 622 9205
Email: carvalho@tstt.net.tt

Trump Luxury Tours & Taxi Service
Crews Inn, Chag
Tel: 634 2189

Vendryes Travel Ltd
71 Frederick Street, Port of Spain
Tel: 623 7272

Winston Nanan-Nanan's Bird Sanctuary Tours
Bamboo Grove Settlement
Valsayn
Tel: 645 1305

Yaron Tours & Travel
31A Lord Street, San Fernando
Tel: 657 1677

WATER SPORTS

Aquamarine Dive
Blue Waters Inn
Tobago
Tel: 660 4341

Black Rock Divers
Le Grand Courlan
Tobago
Tel: 639 0191

Dive Tobago
Pigeon Point, Tobago
Tel: 639 0202

Extra Divers
Crown Point
Tel: 639 7424
Speyside
Tel:660 4852
Email: extradivers@tstt.net

Frontier Divers Ltd
Sandy Point Beach Club
Tobago
Tel: 631 8138
Email: dougdives@tstt.net.tt

Man Friday Diving
Charlottville
Tobago
Tel: 660 4676

Ocean Experience
Pigeon Point Road
Tobago
Tel: 631 8430

Proscuba Dive Center
Rovanel's Resort
Tobago
Tel: 639 7424

R & C Divers Den
Spence's Terrace
Crown Point
Tobago
Tel: 639 8120

R&Sea Diver's Company
Toucan Inn
Store Bay Local Road
Tobago
Tel: 639 812
Email: rsdivers@tstt.net.tt

Tobago Dive Experience
Turtle Beach Hotel
Tobago
Tel: 639 7034

Tobago Divemasters
Speyside
Tobago
Tel: 639 4697

Tobago Marine Sports
Arnos Vale Hotel
Tobago
Tel: 639 4629

Wild Turtle Dive Safaris
Pigeon Point
Tobago
Tel: 639 7936